To June & Graham,   1990.

        aha

61. Vicarage Rd

From Mowlems,   con W.

John Mowlem's
SWANAGE

John Mowlem's
SWANAGE
DIARY ✦ 1845-1851

Edited by *David Lewer*
with an
Introduction and Commentary

dpc DORSET PUBLISHING COMPANY
AT THE WINCANTON PRESS, NATIONAL SCHOOL,
NORTH STREET, WINCANTON, SOMERSET BA9 9AT

John Mowlem [1788-1868]. Portrait by Ramsay Richard Reinagle R.A., 1823. He was employed in 1826 by the Academy to restore da Vinci's cartoon 'Holy Family and St Anne'. In 1848 he was forced to retire from the Academy for having exhibited as his own work a picture which he had bought and not painted. He painted landscapes and was associated with Constable (R.A. 1829), painted his portrait and claimed him as a pupil. He possibly turned to portrait painting to earn a living — whether he was still entitled to use 'R.A'. is not clear.

Published by Dorset Publishing Company at the Wincanton Press, National School, North Street, Wincanton, Somerset BA9 9AT. First published 1990.

Copyright David Lewer © 1990

Typeset by Reg Ward at Holwell, Dorset, and output by Wordstream Limited of Poole.

Layout and design by Rodney Legg.

Printed by Wincanton Litho at Wessex Way, Wincanton, Somerset.

ISBN (International standard book number) 0 948699 15 9

DEDICATION

To the happy memory of Kenneth Burt

John Mowlem's granite column, commemorating King Alfred's naval battle with the Danes in Swanage Bay, A.D. 877.

Contents

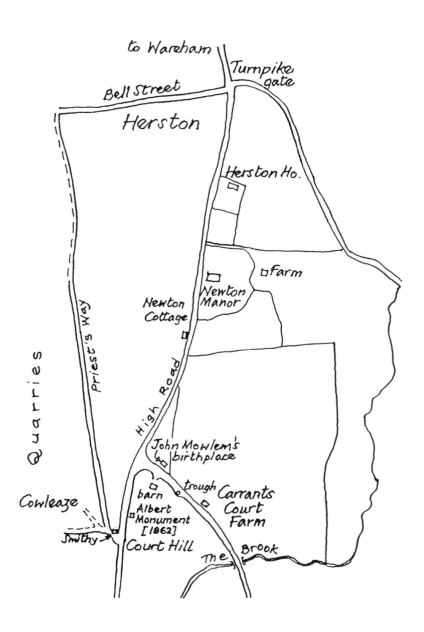

to Wareham

Turnpike gate

Bell Street

Herston

Herston Ho.

Quarries

Priest's Way

High Road

□Farm

Newton Manor

Newton Cottage

John Mowlem's birthplace

Cowleaze

barn

trough

Carrants Court Farm

Albert Monument [1862]

Smithy

Court Hill

The Brook

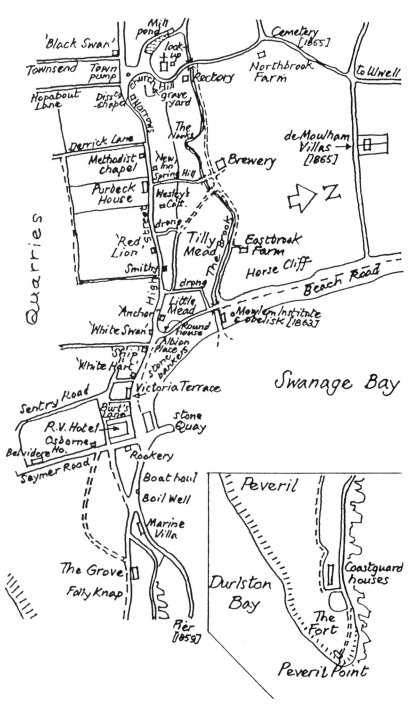

SWANAGE MAP, page 9

MOWLEM family

Alexander   b.1622 Studland
John   b 1650
Alexander   1684 - 1738
John   1715 -? 1799
                         m.1782
John   1751 - 1837 = Hannah FROOM 1764 - 1836 of Ulwell Mill

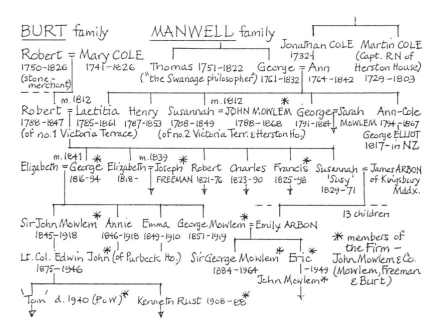

Sarah	Elizabeth	JOHN = Susannah	Joseph ('Mexico Joe')	Robert	James
1784 -	1786-90	MOWLEM | MANWELL	1791-1856	1793-1850	1797-?
= George		1788-1868 | 1788-1849	= Sarah	- Martha	= Jane
MANWELL		(no issue)	WARREN	HIBBS	COLEMAN
					to NY
					1833

m.1812 (above JOHN = Susannah)

John	4 daus.	Thomas Joseph = Elizabeth	Charles	Henry Hibbs	Frank
1817-49		1833-92 | RABLING	d.1859	1817-74	d.1846
d. in Mexico	(unmarried)			= Sarah MANWELL	

Susannah	Louisa	John Ernest - b. Herston Ho.
1861-1935	1864-1940	1868-1946

all lived at de Moulham Villa · Swanage
(no issue)

John (NZ branch)
1840 - ? - r
Arthur Rainsford FRCS 1902-86
inherited Swanage estate · left to Town

☆

BURT family   MANWELL family   Jonathan COLE   Martin COLE
                                         1732†   (Capt. RN of
Robert = Mary COLE   Thomas 1751-1822   George = Ann   Herston House)
1750-1826 1741-1826   ("the Swanage philosopher") 1761-1832 \| 1764-1842 1729-1803
(stone-
merchant)
          m.1812   m.1812   ✳
Robert = Laetitia   Henry   Susannah = JOHN MOWLEM George = Sarah Ann-Cole
1788-1847 \| 1785-1861 1787-1853 1788-1849 1788-1868 1791-1864 \| MOWLEM 1794-1867
(of no.1 Victoria Terrace) (of no.2 Victoria Terr. & Herston Ho.)   George ELLIOT
                                                                        1817 - in NZ
     m.1841 ✳   m.1839 ✳
Elizabeth = George Elizabeth = Joseph Robert Charles Francis Susannah = James ARBON
1816-94   1818-   \| FREEMAN 1821-76 1823-90 1825-98 'Susy'   of Kingsbury
                                                           1829-71   Mddx.

                                                          13 children
                                                          ⌐ ─ ─ ─ ─ ─ ─ ─ ¬
Sir John Mowlem Annie Emma George Mowlem = Emily ARBON
1845-1918   1846-1918 1849-1910 1851-1919

                                                          ✳ members of
Lt. Col. Edwin John (of Purbeck Ho.) Sir George Mowlem Eric ✳   the Firm —
1875-1946   1884-1964   1-1949   John Mowlem & Co.
                                      John Mowlem ✳   (Mowlem, Freeman
                                                                  & Burt)

Tom d. 1940 (P o W) ✳   Kenneth Rust 1908 - 88 ✳

Foreword

I first came upon John Mowlem's fascinating Swanage Diary some twenty years ago. My good friend and neighbour, the archaeologist J. Bernard Calkin, MA FSA, was collaborating with me in writing *Curiosities of Swanage*, and a relative of his chanced to see a typescript of a *History of John Mowlem & Co.* when he was on business with the firm.

This scholarly history had recently been compiled by Frank Baines, author, one time Chindit and colourful man of parts. He was the son of Sir Francis Baines KCVO [1877-1933], architect and director of the Office of Works.

Unfortunately this comprehensive tome was found altogether too long for publication. But by kind permission we were able to borrow one of the half-dozen copies of the typescript, and found embedded therein a transcript of John Mowlem's *Swanage Diary* [1845-51].

The diary itself belonged to Kenneth Burt, the last member of the family to have been a director of the firm. I was fortunate to become a dear friend of this delightful and courteous great-grandson of George Burt, the "King of Swanage", as Thomas Hardy called him, late of Purbeck House, who was a nephew by marriage of John Mowlem and his partner. Kenneth Burt long hoped to see the diary published, but sadly he did not live to see it in print, having died in 1988, like John Mowlem in his eightieth year. Frank Baines, too, died in 1987, and Bernard Calkin earlier in 1972.

Kenneth Burt wrote in 1981: "The original MS is full of character and is in old John's really rather good hand ... He used a largish book bound in rough vellum, which began life evidently as a copy letter book, and later became a sort of 'common-place' book − one finds a poem that took his fancy, and on another page a list of the Cabinet of the time of Lord John Russell, and so on ... I am particularly pleased to have it, because for me it is a sort of background to a continuity which spanned 150 years, and I believe this tradition of quality and fine craftsmanship is still being maintained." In his last letter to me in May 1988 he wrote: "I am so very glad to think you are putting the old man on 'our mutual local map' − it's quite a little epic in its way, and it is in a sense *alive* and shows how society gets built ..."

Unfortunately the original diary is now missing, one hopes only temporarily. But to lessen the disappointment a second diary has recently come to light, and a photostat of its first page is included which shows John Mowlem's 'good hand', as Kenneth Burt has said.

This later diary was a record of John Mowlem's holiday on the continent with two lady companions during the summer of 1853, after his wife's death, which is again not only amusing but also full of interest. As the earlier diary ends abruptly at the very last page of the book it seems possible, even probable, that he continued his journal in an intermediate book. If that ever turns up it would indeed be a happy event.

John Mowlem wrote on 9 September 1850: "I have been a whole week without writing in this book. The reader will say some day this is of little consequence. But I please myself, as it is not for the world, it is as it is."

He comments: "Rude as I am in my speech and little blessed with the soft phrase of peace, yet, by your gracious patience, I will a round unvarnished tale deliver." [Othello].

Always aware of the elements, he records: "The tempest howled, the lightning flashed, the waves ran mountain high. The sky when not illumined by the electric flashes, was black as pitch, and all sails were furled, while the ship was on her beam-ends. Yet I did a mariner's duty."

Then again, perhaps irritated by stupid or dishonest people, he exclaims: "Nero fiddled while Rome was in flames ... "

Finally, and sinisterly: "Lead me to my dungeon!"

In editing and commenting on John Mowlem's diary I acknowledge with thanks all those who have shown interest in the project, and the assistance given me especially by Mr and Mrs Kenneth Burt, David Carpenter — of *London John* [Mowlem's house journal], Frank Baines, J. Bernard Calkin, Sister Mary Liam, formerly of the Convent of Mercy, Purbeck House, whose thesis on similar lines was a happy coincidence, and David Haysom, Curator of the Swanage Tithe Barn Museum, who has prepared the illustrations. The map and *dramatis personae* have been devised by the editor. A very few diary entries which are either repetitive or of minimal interest are omitted.

David Lewer
Swanage
March 1989

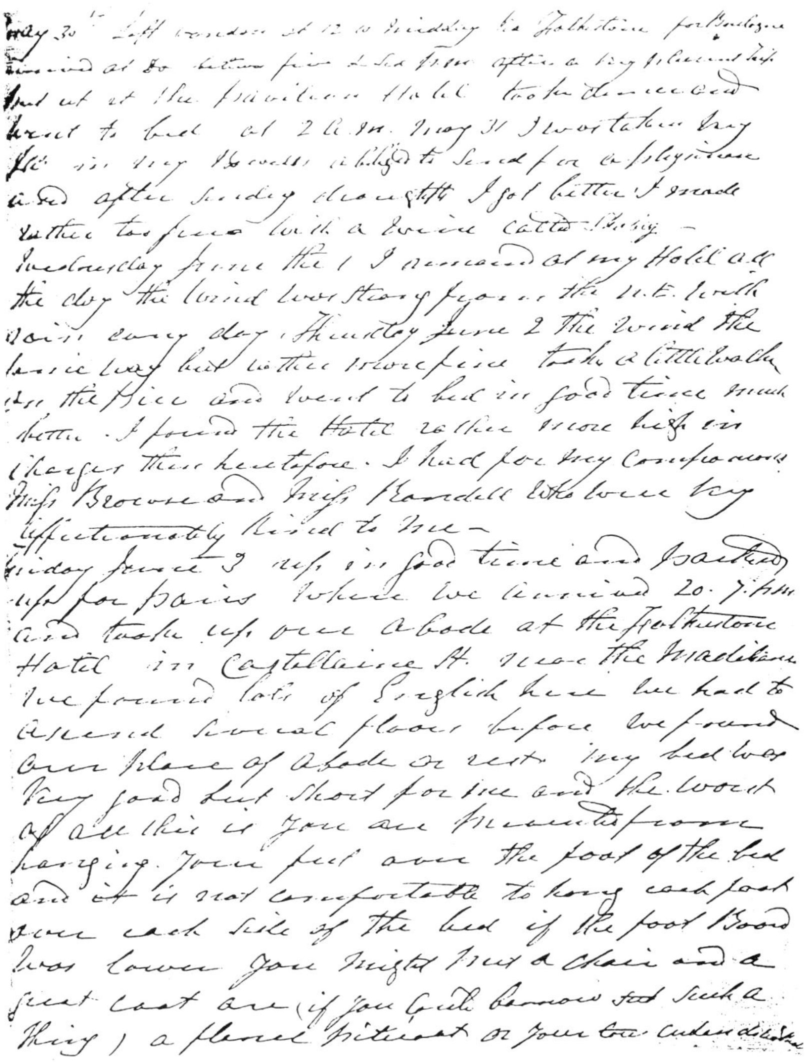
May 30th Left London at 12 o'clock midday via Folkstone for Boulogne
arrived at do. better fine & sea from after a very pleasant trip
put up at the Pavilion Hotel took dinner and
went to bed at 2 a.m. May 31 I was taken very
ill in my bowels obliged to send for a physician
and after sending draughts I got better I made
rather too free with a wine called [illegible] —
Wednesday June the 1 I remained at my Hotel all
the day the wind was strong from the N.E. with
rain every day. Thursday June 2 the wind the
same way but rather more fine took a little walk
on the Pier and went to bed in good time much
better. I found the Hotel rather more high in
charges than heretofore. I had for my companions
Miss Browne and Miss Randell who were very
affectionately kind to me —
Friday June 3 rose in good time and started
up for Paris where we arrived 20. 7 pm
and took up our abode at the Folkestone
Hotel in Castellaine St. near the Madeleine
we found lots of English here we had to
ascend several floors before we found
our place of abode or rest. my bed was
very good but short for me and the worst
of all this is you are prevented from
hanging your feet over the foot of the bed
and it is not comfortable to hang each foot
over each side of the bed if the foot board
was lower you might put a chair and a
great coat are (if you could borrow such a
thing) a flannel petticoat or your own under[illegible]

The first page of John Mowlem's 1853 continental diary.

The boat haul, Swanage Bay. Aquatint by William Daniell, 1823.

Carrants Court, John Mowlem's birthplace, photographed by Walter Pouncy. The family's cottage is opposite the horse and trap. 'Ivydene' further down the hill is in 1989 the only surviving building.

Introduction

John Mowlem was born on 12 October 1788 in an ancient cottage at Carrants Court [Court Hill], Swanage, and died on 8 March 1868, in his 80th year at Old Purbeck House.

William Masters Hardy, the builder and chronicler of *Old Swanage* [1910] wrote of John Mowlem's "romantic career", recalling the half-fabulous story of Dick Whittington: "Such lives can never fail to be read with deep interest, showing as they do what can be accomplished by dint of ability and energy, combined with favouring fortune. Certainly one discerns in the life of such a man as John Mowlem an element of luck as well as pluck − two elements which, united, form a powerful coalition."

John Mowlem wrote [17 May 1847]: "I was one of six children, we were two girls and four boys, a father with no one that could give or lend a penny to hard times for us all. Thank God it is not so now; all a man could wish for I have at my command."

It is more than probable that all the Mowlem children − and their friends, the Burts and Manwells − came under the influence of the celebrated Dr Andrew Bell, who was Rector of Swanage [1801-09] and who introduced the Madras System of monitorial schooling. But John was approaching thirteen years of age when Bell arrived, and may already have started work. Child labour on the farms and in the quarries was universal because it was cheap. However, several small Sunday schools had been established by William Morton Pitt, the philanthropic MP for Dorset. And there was also Thomas Manwell [1751-1822], "the Swanage philosopher"; his niece became John Mowlem's wife. John must have acquired some sort of education and could write and express himself well, as can be seen from his diary, though much of it must have been self-taught or gained through experience.

So, according to Hardy, a poor quarry boy, his three brothers and their father were the last gang of quarrymen who worked at Tilly Whim, which was closed about 1812 following the "slump" towards the conclusion of the Napoleonic Wars. However, it will be seen that by 1808 John Mowlem was in London. His father had a friend, Robert Burt, another Swanage quarrier, who carried on a stone, coal and bakery business and then established himself as a stone merchant. Hardy tells us that Mr Mowlem kept a general goods shop in the west wing of a "picturesque old-time residence with a grand old balcony supported on round stone pillars and caps". This was on the site of

The Round House and Albion Place (right) where John Mowlem senior kept a shop.

Albion Place in the "Square". The portico appears to have been enclosed at some time to form a shop.

Just as John Mowlem senior had a son John, so Robert Burt had a son Robert, and the lads were of the same age. In the year of Trafalgar they were approaching seventeen, and no doubt the two young friends did their courting together, for they married two sisters, Susannah and Laetitia Manwell. They were relatives of Captain Martin Cole RN, of Herston House, which lay on the north side of the high road beyond Newton Manor, also formerly owned by the landed Cockram family.

The Manwells lived at the foot of Church Hill opposite the old rectory, in one of a row of cottages since demolished, the site now forming part of the north churchyard. Sometimes the Manwell girls were at Herston House and it was there, in the adjoining paddock, that the young John Mowlem, and his friend Robert Burt similarly, began to whistle for his wife, as described in the diary.

But young John's thoughts were on a career before marriage. It is possible that the girls' brother, Henry Manwell, gave him the idea of leaving Swanage, for in 1804 at the age of seventeen, Henry went to Portsmouth as a stone-cutter on government works, and then to Calshot Castle. He revisited Swanage at the end of 1806 before resuming work in Greenwich and later at Woolwich Arsenal. It seems likely that he told John of the opportunities for enthusiastic lads in wider horizons, and even may have told him of the possibility of work in the Isle of Wight; he himself was going to London. In the event, John Mowlem "left Swanage with his tools on his back, to seek his way in the world, he being seventeen years of age".

John probably arrived in London in 1807 with rather more than the legendary "ninepence in his pocket". Hardy says that he found a vessel loaded with stone for London, and asking the captain to take him aboard, obtained a free passage. But this does not accord with George Burt's account of his uncle's career, given in a speech at the Mowlem Institute in February 1881, which is to be preferred. According to his nephew, John Mowlem did not go direct to the metropolis but first found employment at Norris Castle in the Isle of Wight, and in due course was recommended by the architect there, James Wyatt, to Henry Westmacott, one of two brothers who were sculptor-masons in London. They lived in Mount Street and shared a workshop in King's Row, Pimlico. In an adjoining house John Mowlem first lodged as a journeyman.

Henry Westmacott had a fashionable practice and had contracts at Kensington Palace, Somerset House, Greenwich Palace and the Royal Mews, Charing Cross. In 1816 John Mowlem was made foreman over all the works then going on in London. "I was put over men old enough to be my father. It is true I knew but little, but I moved upwards, knowing I could any day go back to the bankers [stone quays at Swanage]." Of Westmacott: "I did all I could for his benefit; I never wronged him of a farthing in my life, but his imperious spirit could never meet me freely and manly. He always appeared above his business, except in giving a receipt for money. I would only copy him in two things, cleanliness and punctuality. Very soon after I left him he gave up his business, which he need not have done if he had been liberal enough to have given me enough to live on. I wish him well."

John Mowlem was not one to have his head turned by the novelty of London, nor did he forget his Susan. Perhaps he returned to Swanage, and Laetitia and Susannah Manwell may have visited their brother Henry in London; their other brother George also came up to the metropolis as a stonemason.

In 1812 John and Susannah were married in London. Years later he wrote in his diary: "29 February 1848. This is my wedding day. It is 36 years since I took unto myself a wife. It was a Saturday. We were married at St George's, Hanover Square. Since that time I have had to think deeply how to get a living. We went to live in Pimlico, and I was employed by Mr Henry Westmacott, Government mason. I was his foreman for about seven years. But he was a shabby master ... I remained with him for beggarly wages, knowing that I should be better off one day. My wife had to work with myself. On we went and here we are!"

In the same year, 1812, John's friend Robert Burt duly married Letty Manwell in Swanage parish church. They now began to raise a family of six children, George [1816], Elizabeth [1818], Robert [1821], Charles [1823], Francis [1825] and Susannah Ann – "Susy" [1829]. It was George Burt who was destined to become "King of Swanage". Their father, Robert Burt, did not join the emigration to London but remained in Swanage at the family's expanding coal-and-stone business in the High Street. Similarly Robert Mowlem, the third son of that family, remained at home to look after their quarry, and in 1815 he married Martha Hibbs who came from another quarrying family. They had seven children, of whom the second son, Henry Hibbs Mowlem, married Sarah Manwell, a niece of Susannah and Laetitia. It was their son John who was taken up by his great-uncle and namesake, and sent to school in Guernsey; he later emigrated to New Zealand where he died leaving a large family. John Mowlem's interest in his great-nephew arose since he and Susannah had no children of their own; sadly she became chronically ill after their marriage.

The establishment of the firm of John Mowlem and Company first appears in a public document in 1823, in the minutes of the Vestry of St George's, Hanover Square. The reference is to do with the paving of roads – something with which he was to remain connected all his life. In those days £100 capital was enough to start a business, and he was helped on the ladder to success by professional friends, who included the Cadogans, father and son, surveyors to the parish of St Clement Danes; Burstall, a builder and surveyor to the parish of St Martin-in-the-Fields; Ponsford, an architect-builder and speculator in house property; and perhaps most important, the McAdams of road-making fame. As soon as he had started work on his own, John Mowlem took a lease of a wharf in Pimlico Basin, now the site of Victoria Station forecourt, where he imported Purbeck limestone, York sandstone and Aberdeen granite.

Meanwhile Henry Manwell, after some years as a stonemason, then as a schoolmaster in London under the wing of Andrew Bell and his Madras System, was elected rate-collector of the parish of St Marylebone. Probably through his brother-in-law, John Mowlem moved his offices and yard to Paddington Basin, off the Grand Union Canal, which remained his headquarters for the rest of his life. Frank Baines discovered that at first John and his wife occupied a house nearby but they later moved to Milton Street, Dorset Square, then in 1831 to 6

Victoria Terrace, photographed by Thomas Powell. John Mowlem's front door (No. 2) is in line with the lamp-post. The date is 1890 though the view had hardly altered from 1850. The old cottage on the corner of Burt's Lane was the birthplace of both George Burt and William Masters Hardy.

Chester Place, a small Nash terrace originally facing Regent's Park. By 1838 they may have moved back to Wharf Road, Paddington; John's youngest brother James Mowlem was occupying the house in 1827 but in 1833 he emigrated to New York.

The second brother, Joseph, had also come up from Swanage and was living in Pimlico in 1828; soon afterwards he emigrated to Mexico as an engineer ("Mexico Joe"), but returned to England for a year in 1833 when his second son Thomas Joseph was born. Robert Mowlem, the third brother, was the only one to remain in Swanage.

Then George Manwell, brother of Henry, Susannah and Laetitia, and who married Sarah Mowlem, also came up to London and became Government Mason [1830-40]. No doubt he put some useful work in Mowlem's way, but John prospered chiefly by shrewd but honest application to secure contracts for the repaving and kerbing of London streets, the responsibility of various parish vestries. Their minutes are full of reference to Purbeck "squares" and "pitchers". But his first really big job was the contract gained for repaving Blackfriars Bridge with Guernsey granite setts as recommended earlier by James McAdam. Little did John think that one day his firm would rebuild London Bridge!

The *Rose* steamer at the Quay, before the first pier, drawn by Philip Brannon, 1858. Also seen are Victoria Terrace, The Royal Victoria Hotel. the Rookery, Belvidere, Marine Villa and The Grove.

As soon as he had secured the Blackfriars contract, he found difficulty in procuring the Guernsey granite, so he decided to obtain his own. "I immediately fixed on a field, all good blue granite, about an English acre, in the NE part of the Island, and to put an end to all disputes paid down the money before I commenced work ... I have an excellent prospect with a head of stone about 60 feet long and 16 feet high, and a smith's shop built thereon. Also a new road made 300 feet long, and as many men as I can possibly place in the Quarry. I am sure of success for I remain on this bleak hill all day, where I am determined to remain − all day long except Christmas Day, and then I was like a fish out of water − until I have completed the job, or at least quarried the stone."

Last but not least of the party from Swanage was George Burt. He came up to London in 1835 at the age of nineteen, at the behest of his uncle, who already appreciated his nephew's "good business qualities, shrewdness, fine character and energy of nature" [Hardy], and saw that he would be an asset to the firm. Moreover, like his uncle, young George had learnt to handle a stonemason's tools the hard way − in the Swanage quarries.

Another experienced stonemason, Joseph Freeman, from Yorkshire had also joined the firm, and in 1839 he married George Burt's sister Elizabeth. So while John Mowlem was in Guernsey he left the business in London to "my two young men". He wrote to George: "I am glad you are at your post and well, and if you can give Joseph a little relaxation I shall be pleased, as he has had enough of it this year. I hope by this day week I shall be able to report progress this side of the Channel. I have a hole bored today about 6 ft deep in the quarry

... I have five stone dressers, all that I can get, at high wages too; but the sun will soon be higher, and some will dare cross the Channel, though it is no joke to do that now ... I have sent to Swanage and am going to send to Dartmouth." He shipped all the granite for Black-friars Bridge by the end of June 1840 and then set sail for London.

Although not yet fifty, John Mowlem had retirement to Swanage in mind. William Morton Pitt had owned a considerable amount of property in Swanage when he died bankrupt in 1836. The Chancery sale took place on 16 August 1838 at the Royal Victoria Hotel, which he bought in 1823 and had created from John Dampier's Mansion as the Manor House Hotel. The sale included the Hotel itself, the Quay, Marine Villa, Sentry Field, Seymer Place, the Watch and Preventive Station, Durlston Quarries, Whitecliff Farm and much else.

According to a jotted-down list in one copy of the printed particulars, "Mowlam" made a bid of £260 for Belvidere No.1, a seven-bedroom house built by Pitt at the top of Seymer Road. However, Cleall's bid was £270, but in the event there was no sale for this lot. If this was John Mowlem's offer, which it probably was, it suggests that he did not buy No.2 Victoria Terrace until after the Pitt sale in 1838. The plot of land in "Mrs Colson's garden" in the lower High Street was situated next to Cliff Place and lay between the White Hart [later the Purbeck Hotel] and a picturesque old house west of the Victoria Hotel, and occupied by Robert Burt senior since 1803.

Peveril Point and the Fort, drawn by Philip Brannon, 1859. The coastguard houses are on the left.

In 1835 Messrs. Burt and Hussey purchased the freehold and began to erect "five Lodging Houses" thereon. The east wall is inscribed "Burt's Place 1835", and when building was completed Robert Burt moved into No.1 with his family. The ceremony of laying the foundation of the westernmost house took place in September and was carried out by William Williams Esq. "The House, which is the property of Mr Hussey of this place, will be of the first-rate character. Situation admirable." The British and Foreign Temperance Society met in "Mr Hussey's large room" on 28 April 1836. In September 1836: "Two of the three excellent lodging houses recently begun in Victoria Terrace are now quite finished, and the third is in progress of completion." The Terrace was named after Princess Victoria, and the Hotel had been similarly renamed, by royal permission, following her overnight stay there with her mother, the Duchess of Kent, on 8 August 1833.

No. 1 Victoria Terrace, Robert Burt's home, showing the original shop windows. It is now (1989) the White Horse Inn. The rendering has unfortunately been removed from the elevation. Top of London street bollard in right foreground.

The upper High Street and the Black Swan, on the right, photographed by B.J.K. Rives.

On 29 May 1837 to celebrate her majority there was "a magnificent display of colours " at the Fort, Coast Guard and Customs House as well as on the vessels in the Bay, when the church bells were rung. On 27 June the churchwardens proclaimed the new Queen. "Great interest was excited from the circumstances of Her Gracious Majesty having once honoured this retired and beautiful watering-place with a visit." Several hundred people formed a procession at Church Hill and marched down the High Street to the Coast Guard Station where three volleys were fired, "the children singing, joined by all the people, both the National Anthem and Rule Britannia ... A brilliant assemblage of ladies added greatly to the scene."

At the opening of Victoria's reign, Swanage was little more than a village, and the population of the parish numbered only some 2,000 souls. The one long street, stretching a mile from the Herston turn-pike to the Quay, passed on the way Newton, Carrants Court Hill, Priest's Way which joined it at the upper smithy [later Parker's Stores], the Black Swan and the Town Pump. At this point Townsend and Hopabout [Upabout] Lane led up to the quarries, while Church Hill dropped down past the Mill pond, the parish church and Rectory to the "lake", then up to Northbrook and so to Ulwell and Studland.

Resuming the descent, the High Street became "the Narrows", then wider at Jubilee Square and Derrick [later Chapel] Lane which led up

Church Hill and Town Pump. The lower cottages were bombed and became the site of the post-war Rectory.

to the Common Fields and the quarries there. Beyond the New Inn and old Purbeck House, the street dropped steeply past "John Wesley's Cottage", the "drong" by Frogwell [later the Town Hall], the Red Lion, the smithy and the Anchor to the Round House or Square. Round the corner the strand [later Institute Road] led to Tilly Mead, the County Bridge and the north shore. Inland past Eastbrook Farm was the Brewery [now, amusingly, the site of the Health Centre].

From the Square the lower High Street embraced the Ship Inn and led past Victoria Terrace and Burt's Place to the Royal Victoria Hotel. Behind the latter was Marshall Lane leading to Osborne House, the Rookery — the Library and Customs House — and to Seymer Road which climbed to Belvidere and Sentry fields. Beyond the Quay were the boat haul, Boil Well, the "Hotel Park" — on former quarry land — and the bridle way over Folly Knap, past "The Grove", newly built by Mr Coventry, and so to the Preventive Station and the Fort at Peveril Point.

It seems that John Mowlem began his diary as soon as he had arrived back in Swanage and moved into No.2 Victoria Terrace. Although five houses were mentioned when first being planned, there are only four, and his was double-fronted; the balcony railings are also more decorative. Originally there were no shops in Nos. 2 and 3 as there are now. When he decided to make Victoria Terrace his home it was no doubt arranged for the new building to take in two of the houses. The rooms are spacious, and the impressive staircase leads up to his "observatory", a four-windowed turret set over the roof, with a fine view of the Bay and the "bankers", the piles of stone which in those days were stacked along the shore from the Quay to the brook, awaiting sale and to be shipped up or down the Channel.

So here in November 1845 were John Mowlem and his wife back in their Swanage birthplace. In January the firm had become "Mowlem, Freeman and Burt", but John Mowlem was still very much the senior partner and surprisingly mobile from such a remote spot, though the first railway was about to enter Dorset, from Southampton, bringing a station to Wareham [1847], and Guernsey was accessible, if perilously sometimes, by sailing-ship.

The firm's total stock in 1845 was valued at over £5,000 but by 1850 it had doubled. An inventory at head office gives: 2 desks, 2 tables, (1 new, value £2), 5 stools, 7 chairs, 1 brass candlestick, 1 double japan ditto, 1 coal scuttle & scoop, 1 candle-box, 27 japan boxes for papers, 8 ink stands, 4 rulers, 1 letter stamp, 1 set of fire-irons, 2 iron chests, 1 letter-weighing machine and weights, 1 portable stove, 1 pair of large scissors, 6 knives and forks, 1 corkscrew, 2 drawing boards, 1 alma-

The Narrows, now the widest part of the High Street. All the buildings on the south side were demolished following war damage.

nack, 1 umbrella stand, 3 measuring tapes, 1 measuring chain, 1 barometer, 1 Union Jack, 1 plan of St Martin-in-the Fields, 1 map of England & Wales, 1 map of Guernsey, 1 clock, 5 directories, 1 wash hand basin, 1 looking glass, 1 set of shoe brushes (3 each), 2 clothes brushes & hat brush, 1 hearth broom, 1 long handle broom, 1 door mat, 2 pieces of coconut fibre matting, 1 book bag, 5 towels, 3 dusters, 2 table-cloths, 18 plates, 3 cups & 1 saucer, 1 teapot, 1 egg cup, 1 milk jug, 1 vegetable dish, 2 wine glasses, 1 tumbler, 1 bread pan and a mouse-trap.

Some years later George Burt followed his uncle's decision to retire to Swanage. In 1857 he bought Purbeck House, a Georgian building on the High Street, where John Mowlem died in 1868. George Burt rebuilt the house in 1875 and would die there in 1894. The family retained it until after the First World War; after being offered to the town and having been rejected, it became in 1935 the Convent of Mercy and School.

Between 1858 and 1860 John Mowlem bought the estate now occupied by most of Swanage north of the brook and extending to Ulwell. During his retirement and following the diary years, he left several Swanage memorials besides his own monument tomb.

The first was his part in the construction of the first pier in 1859. This has all but disappeared.

The second was the famous granite column, still standing on the front. "In commemoration of a great naval battle fought with the Danes in Swanage Bay by Alfred the Great, AD 877." But it is doubtful whether Alfred's fleet played any part in the drama, Peveril Ledge being more likely the cause of the Danish disaster when 120 longboats were wrecked there.

The third was the erection, with his nephew George Burt, of the monument to "Albert the Good", the Prince Consort, in 1862. This column stood on Court Hill but was demolished in 1971 by developers, thereby causing an outcry.

The fourth was the Mowlem Institute, which was opened in 1863 "for the benefit and mutual improvement of the working classes", but for a century became a centre for all the inhabitants and visitors as a library, museum, lecture and meeting hall. It was replaced in 1966 by the Mowlem Theatre.

In January 1865, to celebrate the anniversary of the Institute, a public tea and concert [price one shilling] was held there at which Mr John Mowlem, by then aged 76, sang "Lord Dundreary". There were 360 people present.

The great expansion of John Mowlem & Co. Ltd. [it had reverted to the original name] followed the first large building contract — the rebuilding of Billingsgate Market in 1874. Then came, among many others, Smithfield Market, the City of London School, the British Museum extension, Imperial Institute, Regent Palace Hotel, and the Queen Victoria Memorial. George Burt's son, Sir John Mowlem Burt [1845-1918], was knighted for the preparation of Westminster Abbey for Edward VII's coronation. Subsequent coronation works were continued by the firm including the building of the Westminster Abbey annexe in 1937.

In more mundane areas docks, roads, railways, tunnels, sewers and airfields have been constructed by Mowlem. The London and South-Western Railway's short cut Bournemouth-Poole line was formed in 1886, and the Dorchester bypass would follow in 1988. The total value in contracts 1874-1960 was approximately £190 millions. Since then the firm has grown astronomically, and development has spread world-wide. By the end of the 1980s turnover reached £1,000 millions.

The first and perhaps most elegant skyscraper built after the last war was the Vickers Tower on the site of the firm's former headquarters on Millbank. But perhaps the most sensational enterprises completed in recent years have been the NatWest Tower in the City and of course, the new London Bridge, followed by the London City Airport and Docklands Light Railway.

Mowlem has come a long way from repairing Blackfriars Bridge a century and a half ago and that mouse-trap, yet the spirit of the Founder still seems to hover over the firm's endeavours.

The Mowlem Institute, 1863-1966. Courtesy the Mowlem Theatre.

John Mowlem's observatory on the roof of No. 2 Victoria Terrace (centre) and his view of the Bay. Photograph by B.J.K. Rives.

The Mowlem Institute (1863) and the bankers, photographed by B.J.K. Rives.

The Diary

▷ Throughout there is great emphasis on the weather and the state of the tides. He begins:

Saturday 8 November 1845: Wind SE by S, strong breeze through the day, the barometer low. About 6 p.m. heavy rain with thunder, lightning very vivid which lasted for two hours and then it cleared, with starlight.

Monday 10 November: Wind SW, fine breeze. Ten vessels in the Bay for stone and four Cowes pilot boats, one revenue cutter.

Wednesday 12 November : Wind N by E, light breeze and fine, the mercury on the rise ... walked to the Fort with Mrs Mowlem and Mrs Robert Burt.

▷ Mrs Mowlem is of course his wife Susannah. Mrs Robert Burt is her sister Laetitia, of No.1 Victoria Terrace. The Fort was on Peveril Point. It is described by Philip Brannon in his Swanage Guide [1st ed. 1858]: "A road leads up the hill across Sentry Fields to Peveril Point, passing by the entrance to 'The Grove'." But a lower path, "entered by a wicket between the grounds of the above residence and 'Marine Villa', passes the Coastguard Station and reaches the open sward and beach of Peveril. Clambering over the surge-worn masses of rock and rugged shingle, the traveller will ascend by some steps and rest awhile on the Point. The views of Swanage and the whole bay, the chalk cliffs and hills, and distant shores, are remarkably fine and clear ... Two or three rusty instruments of modern warfare and the deserted circular battery are before him."

Received 4 gallons of gin from London via Poole, and brass rods for dining room from Jones of Rose St., St Martin's, London. When the brass rods was landed the boys on the Quay said it was rockets.

Thursday 13 November:wrote J. Freeman and Thos. Burley who is at 139½ Cheapside having attended the sale of the *Francis Yates* — she was sold to a stranger for £1,200. Mrs Burley is also in London. An eclipse of the moon this night.

▷ Mr and Mrs Burley from Guernsey were business friends of John Mowlem.

Friday 14 November: Fixed brass rods round the dining room with Martin Ellis. Remained in the house all the day. Fog cleared away at 12.

▷ Martin Cole Ellis was a great character. Hardy says that Ellis,as an old man in 1880, got a man with a large spawl hammer and beat down the posts which the Local Board had erected across the Quay. In 1834 he had been sentenced for one month in Dorchester gaol for trespassing.

Old Purbeck House, demolished 1874, photographed by B.J.K. Rives. The summer house at the top of the garden has survived (1989).

Saturday 15 November: Remained all day at home. Put down Turkey carpet, put on rising hinges to dining room with Martin Ellis. Several vessels loading in the Bay.

Sunday 16 November: Blowing very hard and rain. No going to church today, no going out. My brother Robert dined here today, Mr Cole supped here in the evening, quoted several passages of scripture (sublime), spoke slightly of Geology and retired at half past nine, the evening fine and starlit. The storm on the 6th instant set fire to a wheat rick near Bridport. Received invoice from Mr Waugh with bill for carpet fringe and damask for drawing room and dining room.

Monday 17 November: Wrote Mr Brown, Mr J. Freeman and Thos. le Maitre, Jr. of St Sampson's. Received of Mr White 5 tons of coal at 1/4 per hundredweight, gave carman 1/- moving the same through the garden, 4/- to my nephew Charles and H. Mowlem. Received a letter from Thos. le Maitre – several ships loading in St Sampson's; the lowest freight is 8/- per ton cash, some at 8/6.

▷ Mr White is William Grove White, a prominent stone and coal merchant who lived at the Old Bank. He was the son of Lt.Col. White, CB., a veteran of the Peninsular War, who had just died in 1844. He resided for many years at Newton Cottage, and it was to be let [Dorset County Chronicle 30 May 1844] with garden, fruit trees and good views. A photograph appears in William Masters Hardy's *Old Swanage*. It received a direct hit by a bomb on 23 August 1942 with fatal results.

Tuesday 18 November: The *Ranger* schooner delivering coals. I walked in the afternoon and read the rest of the day.

Wednesday 19 November: Blowing a gale with heavy rain. Vessels rolling in the Bay, stone-lighter carried away its mast, the weather very thick. No.16 pilot cutter boarded two brigs at noon off Durlston Head, both in want of pilots, one with the loss of jib-boom. Wrote H.C. Elliot, Joseph Freeman, George Burt and Mr Burley. I walked to the Fort.

Thursday 20 November: Wind S to SW by W, blowing a gale with heavy rain and squalls. Collier unloading though blowing so hard. The boats get on shore by a warp with an anchor let go nearly in-shore. The coals are unloaded close to Boil Well. As there is no demand made by anybody for landing coals or shipping stone, how can a charge be made for anyone hauling up his boat or boats on the same spot? This is a legal question, but God protect the poor from Law and Lawyers. Read the whole evening, in bed before 10 o'clock. After bathing my feet and ankles in salt-water, I find them much better. I have continued this for a week.

▷ Until the first wooden pier was built in 1859 — chiefly by the exertions of John Mowlem — there was only the stone quay built by W.M. Pitt after he had bought John Dampier's Great House [later the Royal Victoria Hotel] in 1823. Before that there was only a stone sea wall acting as a quay extending towards Boil Well, a spring which emerges from the hillside at the "monkey beach". Since olden times it was the landing-place where the monkey-boats came ashore for fresh water and provisions for the ships anchored in the Bay.

Friday 21 November: The *Rose* steamer from Southampton called in the Bay with packages but no passengers, proceeded on to Wey-mouth. I wrote J. Freeman respecting a second supply of granite for the Metropolis.

▷ The *Rose* was one of the earliest steamers to call at Swanage. In the engraving by Philip Brannon [1858] it is shown berthed by the stone quay. In the following year the wooden pier was built, and Brannon revised and republished his drawing to show the *Rose* alongside it [as in *Curiosities of Swanage*].
On 20 March 1839 [Dorset County Chronicle] the *Rose* steamer from Portsmouth "left at 10 o'clock this morning on a trip to Swanage with a large party of friends on board". Excellent cabin and accommodation was reported. Another trip from Poole on 7 August included an "excellent Conservative brass band". In October 1840 there was an advertisement for the *Rose*: STEAM — Weymouth to Southampton and by Railway to

London. [The London and South Western Railway, from Nine Elms to Southampton, was opened on 11 May 1840]. "*Rose* leaves Weymouth on Monday and Friday mornings at 9 o'c for Southampton (calling off Swanage and Yarmouth) and returns on Tuesdays and Saturdays on arrival of the first train from London." In June 1842 "The *Rose* recommenced running from Weymouth to Southampton. By taking the morning train at Vauxhall at 7 o'c to Southampton, the journey to Swanage by the *Rose* can be accomplished in the unprecedented short time of 7 hours." The prices in 1845 from Swanage to Weymouth or Southampton were Saloon 7s.; Forecabin 3s.6d.

Saturday 22 November: I find Harding, paviour of Westminster, owes Mr Manuelle £708.14.10, his debts are about £3,000, this will be a drawback for life. Manuelle's son is appointed assignee. I have stowed away today in the cellar 25 bottles of John Ferguson's best brandy, also 25 bottles of the best gin from Seaver Evans. Walked on the cliff in the afternoon with Mrs M. and her sister Elliot, read part of the evening but was more than ever annoyed with boys and young men in front of the house skylarking. It is the only clean place in the whole street, and there being a light in Walker's window they can see the long ribbons dangling from their hats such as I never saw before, which I presume causes their weak minds.

St Mary's parish church, from the south-east, drawn by W.A. Miles. The church was rebuilt in 1859 except for the tower.

▷ Walker's, Chemist and Druggist, was next door at No.3 Victoria Terrace [1851 Census]; Brannon's 1858 Guide gives E.S. Harman, Chemist, Bookseller and Stationer, and later it was the Post Office.

"Mrs M. and her sister Elliot." Mrs Elliot was née Ann-Cole Manwell, both great-nieces of the late Captain Martin Cole of Herston House.

Sunday 23 November: Strong hoar frost. Went to church with Mrs M., Mrs E., and Susy Burt. We heard a sermon from Mr Cook comparing the life of man to a ship in a troubled sea — a good subject — but Mr Cook is no sailor. Received a letter from J. Freeman, 2nd supply for the Metropolis all right with an order for Lambeth Parish. Sad news from New Zealand, the natives are too clever for the English. Read, and went to bed by ten o'clock.

St Mary's parish church interior, drawn by Julia Colson. It was demolished in 1859.

▷ St Mary's, Swanage parish church, was a much-altered medieval building before it was completely rebuilt, except for the ancient tower, in 1859. The interior walls and ceiling were plastered, with box pews, three-decker pulpit and an organ at the west end of the gallery. During 1841-54 the Rector was J.L. Jackson, MA.

Monday 24 November: Wind N by W, very fine with strong hoar frost, 9 vessels in the Bay, all for stone; there are large demands for stone from this place at the present time; one vessel was laden for

Durlston Bay, one ditto at cliff, this is very remarkable at this season of the year and shows what a demand there is for stone. But I see no improvements in the inhabitants, there is nothing like want with those that can work but not one thinks of old age, public houses are in great request, the manners are more rude than they were 50 years ago, both men and women; this is to be much regretted by all who wish them well.

Tuesday 25 November: Several vessels loading in the Bay. Two schooners in the Bay waiting a tide for the west. In the afternoon I drove a horse and gig from the Anchor to Wareham to meet Mrs Burstall from London per the *Emerald* coach; saw Charles Smith, the captain of the *Hero* at Poole with a cargo of coals. I arrived here, Swanage, at 6 p.m., the coach was late, the roads a disgrace to any man. Opposite the church the men was sit in the high road breaking stones promiscuously brought from some quarry, soft and hard, thin and thick, some as big as a child's head, at another place there was pebbles brought promiscuously from the seaside and shot in the street. Lent Martin Ellis £4 for which I have his I.O.U. Received carpet for drawing room, window curtains and ditto for dining room.

The Anchor, Elijah Vacher inn-keeper. This was the posting inn and is one of the oldest buildings in the High Street.

▷ The Anchor was the posting inn and is one of the oldest Swanage houses. An advertisement [Dorset County Chronicle 7 March 1844] gave: "Anchor Inn to be let, together with stabling, coach house ... with horses, flys, gigs and other stock to be taken at valuation. The above business was conducted for many years by the late proprietor, Mr William Hatchard, deceased." In September it was to be sold by auction. On 11 February 1847 Elijah Vacher took over the Anchor Inn, opening it with a dinner.

There was a report [Dorset County Chronicle 20 June 1844] of a new stage coach — the *Emerald*, Weymouth & London via Southampton, "driven by our old friend Wiltshire, who has during a period of 14 years been coachman on this line of road". The coach was built by Jones of Southampton with all the latest improvements. But for stage coaches the writing was already on the wall.

Wednesday 26 November: Blowing very hard, only the Market Boat loaded today, 2 schooners wind-bound, 8 Cowes pilot boats in the Bay.

Friday 28 November: Wind S, strong, with showers, but mild. Several vessels from the Isle of Wight laying their course into the Bay, some are bound to the west but nearly all run for Studland Bay, as the wind increased as night came. 4 vessels came into this Bay and took a little stone on board. Walked to the Fort alone, read, played whist until 10 o'clock with Mrs Burstall, Mrs Elliot and Mrs M., chatted with my brother Robert who informed me there was a letter from my late brother James's wife but nothing about her children, whether dead or alive. What an odd woman for so fine a man as my brother to marry. I wrote Joseph Freeman and wife, also George Elliot to New Zealand, postage 8d. Passed a good day.

▷ James Mowlem was the youngest brother [born 1797]. He married a local girl, Jane Coleman, and they emigrated to New York in 1833. George Elliot [born 1817] was Ann-Cole's son who evidently had emigrated to New Zealand.

Saturday 29 November: Wrote Smith, *Hero*, to go to Guernsey from Poole offering him 7/6 per ton with good dispatch at both ends. Ships much wanted at this price. Read the life of Wallace and Bruce, also extracts from *Circumstantial Evidence*. Played whist with my inmates as before but did not get to bed before past 10 o'clock, which is unusual.

Sunday 30 November: Very fine. Passed a good night, had my breakfast, washed in cold water here in my Observatory, the sun shining beautifully. At ¼ before 9 o'clock, the blackbird singing as though it was May, the sea as smooth as glass and about 20 vessels on their way from the Isle of Wight. Went to church with Mrs Burstall, Mrs Elliot and Susy Burt. Mr Cole came in the evening full of religion but very little charity, my brother Robert dined with us.

Monday 1 December 1845: Wind strong with rain, heavy sea in the Bay. Paid Mr John Smedmore on account, £15 cheque and one five pound note making £20 on account for work done. Wrote George Burt and Thomas Burley, also H. Elliot to know if the stamp for the ground in Little Mead will do by adding the value of fifty pounds to it, the first piece being £95.15.0 and the second piece being £50.0.0 – £142.15.0.

▷ John Smedmore was a well-known Swanage builder. In 1851 he was 41 and employed three men. H. Elliot may have been Ann-Cole's husband, but neither are listed in the 1851 census. John Mowlem bought Little Mead, a small triangular plot now forming the property between the High Street, the alleyway leading from the present Library, and Institute Road. Later it was Mr White's stone-yard, and the initials WGW may still be seen on the wall of the "drong" [Dorset dialect word for alleyway].

Tuesday 2 December: Strong breeze, 14 vessels bound west, several came back, the wind increased and a heavy sea, several small vessels loading in the Bay, a very high tide – I have never seen one higher here; and in the middle of the day a very heavy ground sea on the Ledge. Wrote Mr George Manwell of Plymouth.

Wednesday 3 December: Wind west, blowing hard, 6 vessels in the Bay all loading. The barometer nearly to rain, the clouds very heavy. Noon: showers, hail, storms, wind which continued until evening, then starlight and cold.

Thursday 4 December: Went to Swanage Vestry for the first time, gave to the poor of the parish twelve ¼ tons of coals at 14½ per cwt., excused Gray and Peter Gover one quarters rent. The coals were ordered of Mr H. Gillingham. A long debate arose respecting John Harden who is insane. At last it was agreed: if not better to be removed to the Asylum forthwith. Walked in the afternoon to see him, I found him rational but mad without a doubt. It is a family disorder. I hope God will protect us from such affliction; it is of all others the most lamentable.

Friday 5 December: Harden is removed from hence to the Asylum. He threatened to kill his wife and children. Wrote to J. Freeman, Mr Burstall, Froon & Son, and H.C. Elliot. Froon & Son has sent the branches o/o candelabra, sconces by way of the Great Western so I presume they are in Wales by this time [Swansea, he fears].

Saturday 6 December: Received a letter from Harriet Manwell, 1/-, it is dated Nov. 4/45, Trinidad. She is well and happy. I am very much troubled with the lumbago, scarce able to get into bed. Wrote a few lines to Joseph Freeman. Mr Cole, my brother Robert, Robert Burt and his wife looked in.

▷ The Manwell family tree is extensive. Sarah Manwell who married Henry Hibbs Mowlem in 1840 was the grand-daughter of Joseph Manwell [1754-1833], marbler. When he died he had 15 children, 63 grandchildren and 24 great-grandchildren.

Sunday 7 December: All went to church except myself, being quite disabled with the pain in my back.

Monday 8 December: Had Mr Wilcox here, he ordered a bran poultice to be put on my back at 6 o'clock p.m. and another at 10 p.m., for a chronick lumbago. I found great comfort and ease from the same but found great difficulty in turning in bed.

Tuesday 9 December: Mr Wilcox called and bleed me, found relief immediately in a small degree. Went to bed at six o'clock very so-so. Mr Travers called wishing me to give cheques for coals for the poor which I agreed to do. My back is still very bad, so much I can scarcely move. All are well in the house and very comfortable.

▷ Dorset County Chronicle 1 May 1834: "On Friday last a party of 27 gentlemen sat down to an excellent dinner at the Ship Inn, complimentary to Mr Travers, on his retaking the Inn. Many excellent songs were introduced."

The Ship Hotel and Round House. Bassum was a later inn-keeper there, following Travers mentioned by John Mowlem.

Wednesday 10 December: I am better after medicine and bran poultice.

Thursday 11 December: Expected a letter from J. Freeman respecting the second order for Metropolis but no answer from anyone except le Maitre. A man by the name of Farewell has sadly committed himself with 15 boys at the Chapel, he is a Methodist preacher, he is dismissed the society, he should be hung. I find he has been a bad fellow for years, ever since he has been a preacher. Received two packing cases from Froon & Son from 136 Strand, one large glass for the west end of drawing room, a cornice for each window, one cornice (gilt) for dining room.

Friday 12 December: Mr Smedmore here with two men laying down the carpet in drawing room, fixing gilt cornices to ditto and dining room, also putting up curtains and fringe to windows.

Saturday 13 December: Several vessels loading in the Bay. More stone shipped than was ever known for the season of the year. The men still working away at the carpet.

Monday 15 December: Gave 71 tickets for coals for the poor by order of the Vestry, William Butler I have appointed to see them weighed and delivered to each person. I have been to Morgan's school for the first time. The boys are well behaved and clean. I have told mine that unless they can swim I will not keep them at school. The coals are not all delivered to the poor yet; Mr Gillingham does not like to have anyone to look over him. There is a large quantity of drain tiles landed on the Quay from the Isle of Wight for Mr Colecraft. I wrote Mr Burley and George Burt. There is no letter today from any person.

▷ In the 1851 census, Thomas Morgan [37] is described as schoolmaster with his wife Harriet [38]. Morgan's school appears in the western half of the town. Henry Gillingham was another stone-merchant. "Mr Colecraft" was Calcraft of Rempstone Hall, the owner of one of the large estates in Purbeck; others were owned by the second Earl of Eldon [1805-54] at Encombe, and the Bankes family of Kingston Lacy, Corfe Castle and Godlingston.

Tuesday 16 December: The carpet finished, two sofas covered with same material as for drawing room curtains.

Wednesday 17 December: Paid William Butler 7/- for seeing the coals weighed to the poor of the parish. Saw Theodore Croft, Robert Dowling and his brother together with a gun, heard the report of the gun, saw a rook fall on the ground of Mr Alexander close to the rookery. Dowling took it up, it was twenty minutes before ten in the morning. They were all there at my garden gate after, and Dowling had the gun in his hand. I wrote to G. Burt a long letter. My back is better and I am in good health thank God.

▷ Daniel Alexander [1768-1846] was the architect who designed London Dock and Maidstone and Dartmoor prisons. He had purchased the Rookery at the 1838 Chancery sale but his son sold it ten years later to Lord Eldon who also bought the Hotel.

Thursday 18 December: Wind SW with rain more or less until noon when it veered to NNW and blew a double reef mains'l. The barometer rose from rain to change. Several vessels in the Bay, close in shore, all taking stone. Gave Mr John Smedmore an acceptance for £40 2 months, J.M. & Co. on account of what I owe him, which I wrote J. Freeman on. Arranged old letters and old receipts all day – never went out. Wind N and blowing strong. I wrote a few lines to George Elliot. In his mother's letter he is 28 years old this day. We all drunk his health in a bumper of wine, also that of his wife and boys.

Friday 19 December: Wind W, strong. Barometer gone back from change to stormy in a few hours. Heavy showers. Several vessels in the Bay, all loading stone, the men wet through, nothing on to keep them dry except duck which is wet through in a few minutes; no improvement, the men have no idea of comfort. Read nearly all the day. Read some of the speeches of the members of the Corn League at Covent Garden Theatre, one by the Rev. Fox, the most splendid I ever read. I have heard he is ... [space – what can he have heard?]. I wrote to J. Freeman and Thos. le Maitre to ship about 500 tons or a little more for the Parks Office of Woods. I find we have 19/4 per yard delivered. This is the best price we have ever had, no piece of granite to be more than 1½″ nor less than ⅓″. I find we have an order for 200 yards for Waterloo Bridge. This will swallow up our stock at Bethnal Green.

Saturday 20 December: This is the shortest day – one more. Thank God we have lived so long in this world. I drove to Wareham this afternoon for Mr Burstall to take him from the *Emerald* coach from London, or rather Southampton. The coach was very late. He brought me 4 dish covers from London ordered by G. Burt. I consider them very handsome. Without the crest and backing I find those 4 covers will cost £16. We arrived at Swanage at 6 o'clock, all safe; passed a happy evening. No cabinet ministry yet formed.

Monday 22 December: Wind SW. Hard frost through Sunday night, now inclined to rain. Strong wind and cold. Called on the Rev. J. Jackson respecting Farewell, the Methodist preacher, and agreed with him that if the rascal went away, to let the matter drop; but if he dared to come here again, to procure a warrant and take him before a magistrate for an assault with an intent to commit a felony. I called on Thomas Strickland and told him what would be done if he returned to Swanage. The party of preachers who examined the boys with whom Farewell had taken liberties, suspended him for 12 months. Of course, he can preach and contaminate again. Now he ought to be acquitted or found guilty. He is one or the other. Paid Morgan 5/6 for schooling for poor boys up to Saturday night last. Gave up my voucher book to Mr Travers containing the quantity of coals given to the poor. No news yet of a cabinet being formed. Poor little Lord John has his work to do.

▷ Lord John Russell became Prime Minister in 1846.

Tuesday 23 December: The re-considered Ministry from Monday's paper:

Sir Robert Peel	First Lord of the Treasury
Sir James Graham	Home Office
Earl of Aberdeen	Foreign Office
Mr W.E. Gladstone	Chancellor of the Exchequer
Earl of St Germans	Colonial Office
Lord Lincoln	Board of Control
Mr Sidney Herbert	Board of Trade
Lord Ellenborough	Admiralty
Mr W. Bingham-Baring	Woods and Forests
Lord Brougham	President of the Council
Marquis of Westminster	Lord Privy Seal
Earl of Stradbroke	Chancellor, Duchy of Lancaster
Sir E. Sugden	Lord Chancellor of England

Wind N, strong, 3 reef mainsail. Two London traders in the Bay but no shipping of stone. Went to the butchers and ordered 30 pounds of beef for the old and poor. The farm near Worth, Solway owner, all the ricks were burnt last night, 12 in number, and some poor cattle suffered. I hear it was insured for £700 and worth £1,400. It is supposed it was the work of an incendiary. Solway has lately bought a thrashing-machine and it is supposed this was the cause of the fire.

Wednesday 24 December: Wind N, fine breeze and a most beautiful day. Lots of poor people here begging for Christmas. We gave beef to [?] people and money to [?].

Thursday 25 December: Wind W. Very fine and mild, much more like spring than Christmas. Dined at Mr Burt's with Mrs M. and Susy Burt, Mr Cole, Mr & Mrs Burstall, Mrs Elliot, Robert Burt and wife, junior; left ¼ before 12 o'clock. We had roast beef of old England and plum pudding. Wrote Joseph Freeman.

Friday 26 December: Wind SW, fine with occasional showers, the barometer at fair with an inclination to ascend. A beautiful rainbow. This is Susy Burt's birthday. She is 16 years old. She is 5′ 2⅞ths high. good figure, etc., etc. She would be taken to be 18 years old from her appearance. I have loved her from childhood. May she be as happy through life as she has ever been. We had a large dinner party, Mr and Mrs Burt and family, George Burt came from London, Robert met him at Wareham with a gig. There was no coach from Southampton therefore he posted it to Wareham with 3 others. He arrived here between 7 and 8 o'clock. We danced and sang and passed a very happy evening, broke up at 12 at night. Mr Cole, Miss Ellis and my brother Robert was of our party, 14 in all.

▷ Susy Burt [1829-71] was the youngest member of Robert Burt's family at No. 1 Victoria Terrace. She was loved by all and died at the age of only 41. There is a memorial brass in the Parish Church. She married James Arbon, the son of James Arbon of Hyde House, Kingsbury, Middlesex, much to J.M.'s disappointment who, it seems, hoped Susy would look after him after his wife's death in 1849. The Arbons' eldest daughter Emily married her cousin George Mowlem Burt.

Sunday 28 December: Wind W by S, strong with nearly a gale, heavy rain. Remained home all day. 4 o'clock p.m. a large barque off the Bay but no pilot on the station from Poole or Cowes. The vessel in consequence is brought up outside Studland Bay; there is at the same vessel a signal of distress flying from her masthead, her mainsail split. She is boarded by the cutter boat *Gertrude* and she is brought up in Swanage Bay. She is from Guernsey for Ilfracombe with a valuable cargo on board. She left Guernsey last night at 5 o'clock. It is now 6 p.m. and more moderate and that rain is over.

Tuesday December 30: Blowing very hard. Superintended a hole for pole for vane NE from my house. Paid Captain James Edwards for the same £1.10.0, and freight 2/6 − £1.12.6. It is a fine span, 50 ft long.

Wednesday December 31: Fine weather. Erected pole with copper letters and anchor, but the stock is not wide enough, it flies off the wind; therefore must take it down again. Walked to the Fort and danced at No.1 and passed a happy day. Paid for the gig to Wareham 17/6.

Thursday 1 January 1846: Very fine, walked out and dined at 2 pm. This is Mrs Burstall's birthday. We have had a good dinner. We danced this evening with all our friends at No.1 and hope to be happy. Everything went off well, my brother Robert danced with Mrs Elliot, we had James Manwell to fiddle for us, went to bed at 12 o'clock. I am grateful to Providence for the blessings I enjoy. May 1846 be as prosperous as 1845 has been.

▷ James Manwell [age 63 in the 1851 census] was first fiddle in the Band. He was a letter carrier and according to Hardy looked after the Herston turnpike gate. Details of the Wareham Turnpike Trust were given [3 April 1845, Dorset County Chronicle]: The tolls were to be let by auction. They produced last year the sum of £1,084 above the expense of collection — Lot 1: Stoborough and Side Gates; Lot 2: Herston and Ulwell Gates; Lot 3: Westport Gate; Lot 4: Northport Gates. A note in 1874 reported that Turnpike gates might not be taken down until August 1876.

Friday 2 January: Saw Mr & Mrs Burstall off in a fly to Wareham on their way to London, all well and happy, the fly to be paid for by me. I had a piece of copper added to the stock of the anchor and fixed my weather-cock; it is of copper and gilt, very pretty and well-proportioned. Nothing like it in Swanage.

Saturday 3 January: Fixed the pole again after taking it down. I think it will answer well. Walked to the Fort a long time, paid Hixon for beer to men for assistance in fixing the pole, 7/1. Also Trakes for Smedmore's men putting down a carpet, etc. Went to bed at 10, it was then overcast and the barometer going down from set fair.

Sunday 4 January: Wind at 8 a.m. S by W blowing a gale. Went to church, Mrs M., Mrs Elliot, George and Susy Burt, returned home, dined with the above and my brother Robert. At twilight Mr Vacher brought me the Shipping Gazette to look at. I saw in a moment something was wrong and after a few moments I saw the *John Mowlem* was lost on Cosy Sands, the crew saved, thank God. She was a beautiful schooner, she would carry 245 tons with a good bold side, she was an excellent sea-boat and in a breeze not one vessel in five hundred would beat her.

She was a rakish-looking craft. She was built in St Sampson's in Guernsey in September 1842 by John Sauvery & Son. She was launched on [?] and she was christened by Susy Burt who was then thirteen years old; she stood on the end of a tar barrel. She was dressed in white with a blue ribband round her waist and her hair curled all round her head. I remarked at the time the sailors and fishermen looked more at her than they did at the vessel. The bottle was attached to the bowsprit with a line, but the moment the dog-shore was cut, that moment she was off and she was too quick for the bottle to overtake her. This was considered unlucky by the onlookers – at any rate, she is gone.

It was a noble launch. I shall never forget the feeling when every man who was under control and behaved well took his station each side of the vessel, not a breath was heard. All was silent as death until the word was given when each wedge was made to feel the hammer and was made tight. Now for a glass all round. When every man took his place as before, the question then was "Are you ready, men?" Answer, "All ready." "Up with her." "Set her up." "Up with her." "Huzzah!". "Hit her up!" when every maul struck at the same instant like a clap of thunder. She was up and hung by the dog-shore. All was ready.

When the word was given "Cut", away she flew into her native element like a dart. I was on board, delighted with all I saw and heard. She looked like a cork on the water. She was and is not.

Monday 5 January: Wrote J. Freeman and T. Burley. Sent two signatures to pay the men in Guernsey on Saturday next. Wrote Captain Fowler to cheer him up after his loss and invited him to Swanage. I find the crew of the *John Mowlem* was picked up by a collier after being in the boat for 12 hours, and landed at Ramsgate. The vessel struck on the Cosy Sands the first day in the year at 8 o'clock at night; but how she got there is yet to be known from the captain, the Cosy Sands being within the Kentish Knock.

Tuesday 6 January: George Burt is gone to Poole in an open boat with his brother Robert, from thence to Gosport by steam via railway to London. His health is improved since he has been here.

▷ The London and South Western Railway line from Bishopstoke (later Eastleigh) to Gosport was opened in 1841.

Mr Jackson called here respecting the blackguard Farewell who is not ashamed to be seen about this place after what has been found against him. There will be a warrant out for him shortly if he does not leave the place.

Thursday 8 January: Called on Mr White, churchwarden, respecting Farewell.

Friday 9 January: Wind south, light air, very fine like summer. Birds singing, primrose and some roses in our garden. Our post did not arrive until late. It was eleven o'clock before we got our London letters. I wrote Col. Maberley in consequence.

Saturday 10 January: Eleven vessels in the Bay for stone. A large quantity of dressed blocks for Southampton Docks sent by Mr White.

Sunday 11 January: Went to church and heard Mr Coulson preach. I had much better have been at home.

▷ The Rev. John Morton Colson [1797-1866] Rector of Peatling Parva, Leicestershire, married Julia [1795-1865]. Their unmarried daughter Julia [1830-1919] was even more formidable and lived at Belvidere. Hearing that a new boy was in her Sunday school, she exclaimed: "The name Burt means Rogue!"

Monday 12 January: Walked to Hurston and in front of the houses there proves what the inside must be. Surely religion has not done so much for the people as I expected. I fear there is too much outward show. I saw some marks on an old tree that I cut when a little baby. The top of the tree finds its age as well as I do mine. I sent for the constable and walked through the street with him in order to take any unseemly person to the lock-up house, but all was still. I suppose the boys got wind of the beak's being out.

▷ John Mowlem always spells Herston as "Hurston". "Herestone" is mentioned in Domesday, as is "Moleham" and "Suuanwic" or "Sonwic". The lock-up, or "Blind House" on account of the lack of windows, had been built in 1803 and stood in the churchyard until 1860. It may now be seen behind the Town Hall. There was so much rowdyism in the street that at a Vestry meeting held on 28 November 1802 it was decided to build a lock-up for offenders. It was agreed "that the House of Confinement be built on the north side of the Church Tower, 5½ feet by 7 feet in the clear; Secondly, that the said house be built by voluntary subscription; Thirdly, that a number of the Parishioners form themselves into a committee for the purpose of enforcing good conduct and regular behaviour consisting of the churchwardens and overseers for the time being".

Wednesday 14 January: Went to the Post Office, saw Mr Hunt of Godlingston, we walked to Mr White's and then to Mr Serrell's the Magistrate [of Durnford, Langton Matravers] for a warrant for George Farewell for his bad conduct.

▷ Godlingston was an ancient manor house and farm on the Bankes Estate, James Hunt being the tenant. The Poole and Dorset Herald [13 May 1847], quoting from Chambers's Edinburgh Journal, said that Mr Hunt, "a Dorsetshire yeoman" was well-known in this county as a curer of stammering. The cure is effected in twenty minutes, but he keeps the means a secret. "He has been called a quack by medical men. A pity."

Thursday 15 January: I caused George Butler to take out 5 summonses for boys who had committed a nuisance at Mrs Hussey's door.

▷ Mrs Hussey was still living at No.4 Victoria Terrace. Her husband James, who built the house, died in April 1842 aged 43, and in June the entire stock of drapery, grocery etc. was auctioned.

The Gaol, Prison, Blind House, Lock-up or House of Correction. It was at first behind the parish church, now behind the Town Hall. Photograph courtesy Dorset County Museum.

Ulwell Mill where John Mowlem's mother, Hannah Froom, was born. Etching by Alfred Dawson in 'Picturesque Rambles in the Isle of Purbeck' by C.E. Robinson, 1882.

Friday 16 January: I have taken up here into my observatory or Tower a cabinet of beautiful workmanship, I presume it is some two or three hundred years old. I should like to know its origin. There were this morning 12 vessels in the Bay and nearly all for stone. Times are good here but the working-man does not thrive — too fond of the ale-house. My brother has called; he does not like the idea of going to Wareham to appear against those who broke his railing down.

Sunday 18 January: Mr Cook preached an excellent sermon — "Quanch not the spirit".

Monday 19 January: Going via Wareham to London if the coach is not full.   ☆   ☆   ☆   ☆   ☆

Saturday 28 February 1846: Returned from London with Mr Henry Cadogan. Came all the way from Paddington without eating anything on the road, arrived here about half past five a.m., with a bad cold.

▷   "… Paddington", i.e. the Wharf, not from the G.W.R. station and not yet built.

Sunday 1 March: I am too unwell to go to church today. My brother Robert has not yet been. He, poor fellow, is much depressed on account of having lost his son Frank. He was taken ill on the Friday and buried the following Tuesday. He had a tooth extracted the day before he was taken ill and my opinion is, the tooth being very large, he caught cold and brought on an ulcerated throat which caused his death. Poor lad, he is out of a troublesome world, there was nothing before him but trouble and hard work. [Frank was the fourth son, born 1829].

Monday 2 March: About a dozen vessels in the Bay, all for stone for Southampton and Portsmouth. My cough is bad indeed, Mr Wilcox has sent me medicine, hope to be better tomorrow.

Wednesday 4 March: Walked to Ulwell with Mrs Mowlem, Mrs Elliot, Susy Burt and H. Cadogan from Essex St., Strand, London. Found it very dirty but fine. We went to admire the beautiful spring water at Ulwell which has been flowing before my grandfather was born. It springs from chalk and this spring drove the mill where my poor mother was brought up — Ulwell, from whence she rode daily to Corfe to school to one Mr Burt, who was a first-rate schoolmaster.

▷   John Mowlem's grandfather, also John, was born in 1719. *His* grandfather John [born 1650] and great-grandfather Alexander [born 1622] came from Studland. J.M.'s mother, Hannah Froom [1764-1836] lived at Ulwell Mill. In the last century Ulwell was an idyllic if perhaps dilapidated hamlet. John

Ernest Mowlem [1868-1946], the last member of the family to live in Swanage, claimed in his privately printed book *Moulham — the Place and Surname* [1934] that he descended from Durandus the Carpenter who took the name de Moulham. King William the First gave Moleham, or Moulham, land south of Godlingston near Swanage, "to be held by service that he should repair the timber work of the great tower of Corfe Castle and clense the gutters as often as need required".

It has been suggested that Durandus actually built the wooden castle. Over 500 years later, in 1598, the tenure of Moulham land still bore the same condition: surely, said Kenneth Burt, a record for continuity in maintenance contracts!

Thursday 5 March: Mrs Burt was going to London via steamer from Poole with her son Robert. Little R. Gillingham offered to drive them in his gig to Brownsea but when he got near Studland he managed to upset the whole party. Mrs Burt was conveyed home in a cart and obliged to go to bed. Her trip to London is in consequence postponed.

Saturday 7 March: Wind all round the compass, very light breeze and sometimes a perfect calm. Walked to the Fort with Mrs M., Mrs E., Susy Burt and Mr H. Cadogan, the sea like glass. Some porpoises off the Ledge were leaping out of the water, all going with the flood tide and at a rapid rate. The sunset as beautiful as June, the birds singing gaily, the rooks building their nests. I received a letter from Mr Joseph Freeman stating we had got St George's paviour's work, also South West District, and the granite of St George's was given to Freeman at 12/10 and 15/10 per ton.

Swanage Regatta, 1888, photographed by Thomas Powell. Although 40 years later than John Mowlem's reference, the scene is little changed. Only the first pier (1859) and the clock tower (1868) are 'new'.

Wednesday 11 March I am going to London today with Mr H. Cadogan. I arrived in 126 Praed St., Mr Joseph Freeman's residence, at 10 p.m., all well.

Thursday 12 March: Attended St Martin's Committee and got the contract for 3 years for foot and carriageway at a good price. I remained in London from this date until 18th instant when I left London to proceed to Hartlepool and Aberdeen. I left by the Birmingham Line of Rail, dined at Derby. This is a fine station indeed. The day was fine until we arrived near Wakefield when the snow came on very fast from the north. When we arrived at York the snow was deep, no rails could be seen and the wind blew hard and right ahead. We arrived at Darlington at half past seven p.m. where I remained all night; was well accommodated with a good bed and that which was good for the inner man − a good beef-steak for tea. The snowstorm commenced at Durham at 6 a.m., and it gradually passed south to London. The thorn blossom looked very dingy when surrounded with snow. On our journey we passed through Leicester, Derby, York and Thirsk.

▷ Kings Cross station and the direct line from London to York were not opened until 1852.

Thursday 19 March: Left Darlington at half past 9 a.m. for Stockton, where I arrived 20 minutes before eleven in the morning of the same day. Waited until 12 o'clock, as there was no engine, the road being blocked with snow. Half-way to Hartlepool the passengers had to find shelter where they could. I arrived at Hartlepool at the King's Head at 1 p.m. where I sent for Captain Fowler, cold with wet feet from the snow at each station. I went to see the new ship through snow and mud as black as ink. I must confess this appeared the dirtiest place I ever saw − filth of every description. I was pleased with the frame of the ship and have no doubt but she will be a fine vessel but she will never sail like the *John Mowlem* built in Guernsey by Sauvery. It appeared to me the new ship would be hollow by the bow. I got very wet in my feet looking at this ship and was more cold than I have been for a long time. The wind was blowing very strong and not a single person at work at any place.

Friday 20 March: 6 a.m. I rose from my bed such as I am not accustomed to sleep on but it was the first inn, therefore it was, I suppose, the best bed. The little drop of water allowed I could neither wash or shave with. I was therefore obliged to look at my hands and face but could not clean either. I look a queer fellow to be so dirty first thing in the morning. Left Hartlepool ¼ after 11 a.m., arrived at Sunderland, which is 20 miles, in a very short space of time – a great distance on an inclined plane where we travelled at a great rate. I did not much fancy the oscillations. We arrived safe and then I had a long distance to walk, the snow was partially melted but the water from the eaves of the houses was like heavy rain. Having waded through the black mud and snow water I arrived at the Ferry, crossed the deep and narrow River Wear and then had to ascend the steep ascent on the north side. There I arrived at another station of rather a superior kind, the passengers on this train was a shade above those at Hartlepool and Sunderland. We were soon hurtled away to Gateshead which is south of Newcastle, the river parting the two places.

As I was seated in one of the first class carriages which was of a very superior description, I thought – if all the Ministers of the Gospel were to preach the inhabitants of the two last places cleanliness, what a different face of beings there would be. But it is all about having a clean heart, never mind the outside of the platter. My opinion is, a dirty fellow cannot worship his God aright. This is not only prevalent in large towns of the north, but it is here in my native place which is full of religion but there are dirty people.

I soon arrived at Gateshead where I took a fly to the Queen's Head, a very short distance, charge 2/-. This is a very large inn and the same I met Mr Stamp at some few years ago. Here I passed my evening and night, took breakfast the next morning March 21st at 7 a.m. and left at 8 a.m. by the *Chevy Chase* for Edinburgh. We had a few outside passengers but full inside, a Scotsman, myself, a Scotch lady of title whose name was Bailey, she was 50, and her daughter who was very ladylike, free and easy, about 25 years of age. She was like Miss Stephens (a famous actress), now Lady Essex.

When we had travelled about 46 miles towards Edinburgh we were overtaken by a tremendous snow storm with a gale of wind. The drifts were frightful. We had nearly reached the top of the highest hill where there was a cutting – in this cutting there were two carts laden with coals, the horses and men were gone and the carts were nearly buried in snow-drift. To pass on either side was impossible, our horses were beaten, one fell down and there the poor fellow appeared quite happy. Our outside passengers were reduced to two young men, our coach to axle-tree in snow drift, to go back was frightful and to go forward appeared impossible. The snow was still falling fast and it was near 3 p.m.

The idea of being there all night was anything but agreeable. The two men, guard and coachman at last got the coach pulled round to go back. I was obliged to alight and lend a hand. I had on a pair of thin boots, having been wet the day before. I did not at all like this.

Just as we were looking to find the way back we saw four carts with earthenware with good horses, and as they were bound forward they made trace horses and took those carts over the brow of the hill and then took our coach the same way. On we moved, some on one side of the coach and some on the other, to prevent the coach from upsetting. This we did with some difficulty and at last we reached Jedburgh where it is usual for the passengers to dine on their way to Edinburgh.

It so happened that the coach from Edinburgh returned back, having approached the hill on the north side, but as the wind was south the passengers all agreed to return to Jedburgh and remain until the weather was more fine. At the moment we arrived, the up-passengers were about to take our dinner. This we would not submit to and entered our protest against it. We had our dinner, warmed ourselves, and then we departed for the far-famed city of Edinburgh which place we arrived at at ½ past 11 p.m., glad enough. We were not expected.

We stopped at the Crown in Princes St., a good inn, full of travellers who appeared very comfortable. I forgot to say that we all paid the guard and coachman more than double fees. I took something to eat, went to bed, slept well, but was very sore from the exertions of the day previous.

Sunday 22 March: Rose at 9 a.m. and got a good breakfast. After this all the city appeared to be on the move to some place of worship, well-dressed and well-conducted. Having seen a view of this city at my much respected friend William Tyler Esq., of the Surrey Zoological Gardens, and having had this view explained, I knew more of the city by far that most strangers would know. When I left my inn I am free to admit I was astonished at the splendour that appeared before me. Carlton Hill I know all about, or nearly so, but when I looked the contrary way I was astonished more than ever, for there I saw a building this most beautiful I had ever yet seen. What can this be? I cannot ask, for everybody must know it, So I stood and stared and looked again, what can this be, I have never heard of it?

"Oh," I said. "this is Scott's Monument! This is something to be proud of, bravo, you Scots, we have nothing like it." I heard it was the plan of an humble individual who has since been found drowned in the canal.

After I had gazed on this until I thought people would laugh at me, I went on the top of Carlton Hill, the city was at my feet and monuments about me, the fine blue river was studded with vessels. I have never seen anything so grand and I have not words to express my feelings; where are the artist, where the navigator?

I next went into the Statuary on the hill. Though not open on Sunday, my simple appearance gained me an admittance, where I feasted my eyes for more than an hour. Here indeed, though in a very rough-shed, was to be seen some excellent sculpture by a native, a Mr Forest.

First is Robert the Bruce on a war horse receiving a poem from the monk Baston, one of the best pieces of sculpture.

> Queen Mary on horseback and Lord Harries urging her to retreat from Langside.
> The Duke of Marlborough and Steed.
> Duke of Wellington leaning on a Flemish horse (very good).
> Mazeppa on a wild horse (beautifully conceived).
> St Paul's conversion, his horse alarmed (this fills you with *Awe*).
> King James on horseback attacked at Crammond Bridge.
> Napoleon and his charger Marengo (I thought little of this).
> Queen Elizabeth addressing her troops at Tilbury (Masculine).
> Charles XII and a Cossack Prince under a tree. (Oak, Very good).

All the Equestrian Groups and Statues are of choice specimens of Scottish stone, all are finished in a first rate style, where to find a place like it in England I know not.

It was near 4 o'clock p.m. and I needed my dinner so after another view I went to my hotel and dined in mixed company, mostly commercial men − some of them rather *fast* but knew what was good − we took our bottles of wine, read a little which brought my bed-time as I had to be off before 5 a.m. by the Aberdeen Mail which took me to Grantham Pier or Queens Ferry. We crossed in a very good steamer, coach, passengers and luggage, no horses. This is a fine piece of sea, good deep water and plenty of room for a sailing match. There is an island in the middle called Inverkeithing with a light-house and a revolving light which was burning when we crossed. We now took fresh horses and on we went gaily with good horses and good roads to a place called Cupar where we had an excellent beef-steak breakfast for 1/9 at McNabs Hotel where you get half an hour to clean up a little. I now travelled outside to the side of the Firth of Tay, a very pretty river, and right before you is that busy and pretty place Dundee. The sun shone beautifully on hill and spire and all appeared life, wealth and bustle (rather dirty).

We crossed this river in two steam boats fastened together. From all I could discover it was a very curious invention, very wide on deck, very well managed and great civility. We were enlivened by a Scotch fiddler who was blind. He gave us several Scotch airs and I observed he picked up a good many pence, and as this boat passes over this Ferry 12 times a day, this poor blind fiddler must be doing well and will soon buy some *estate*. We now, after a beautiful drive, take a railway train along by the side of the River Tay until we come to Arbroath, not so pretty a place as I expected to find, knowing as I do that Henry Westmacott, Esq., resides there. How a man so particular in everything, a man so cleanly in his habits, a man so proud and aristocratical, can pass his life in such a place as Arbroath I cannot conceive. I was in early life his foreman, taken from the number of journeymen to complete a job in Whittlebury Forest at the house of General Fitzroy.

We again left the Railway at Arbroath and took coach to Montrose, Brecchin, Stonehaven, and on to Aberdeen. Stopped at the Royal Hotel, Union Street, where there was a good dinner prepared for those who had travelled and those who were commercial men. Everything was good and in abundance, waiters all of the first-rate dressed like gentlemen. After dinner I strolled out, found the waterside and saw lots of first-rate vessels and a magnificent harbour, took a view of the granite made for the London market and found the stocks as rough there as in London. Walked until I was fatigued, went to my hotel and then to bed not of the first rate and no supply of "crockery", which is rather an awkward affair after taking whisky toddy. This may appear strange but it is true, and the same deficiency occurred the second night. I then spoke of it and the apartment was furnished properly. I will not satisfy you ladies what I did but I managed.

The next morning I took a good breakfast and made myself known to the merchants but gave no order. I went with Mr Nicholl to see the Quarries. He drove me there in a gig and thanks to my stars he did not break my neck. He told me he could drive four-in-hand. I thought this might be true but I saw in a moment he could not drive one-in-hand, for holes and great stones he never looked at and then to mend the matter I saw the horse, which was a very fine animal, was not a little inclined to shy. So said I, my wife will be a widow through this four-in-hand Scotchman. However he put me down at the Royal Hotel, paid the hire and very politely said adieu. This was liberal and well-behaved for a North Briton. The Quarries are very like others in the south only it is granite and the rock is removed and broken with powder. The men at this time are getting great wages in consequence of the great demand everywhere for stone.

I had said farewell to Mr Nicholl, washed for dinner and had just taken my place at the table when who should enter the room but Mr William Freeman of Millbank. He arrived with the same coach from Edinburgh as I did before. As a matter of course, as we knew not of each other being from home, this was an unexpected treat. We sat and dined together and we were very happy and jolly. I had arranged to leave Aberdeen the next morning but I altered my mind and remained with my unexpected friend Mr Freeman until Friday March 27th.

After breakfast we walked forth from our inn and called on Mr John Gibb who is a fine old fellow. He built the granite bridge at Glasgow and after he had commenced, the Committee said it was too narrow by one third and what would be the extra charge to make it that one third wider? He said, "One third more money, of course!" They said "Very well", and closed the bargain. Everyone must know this was a good day's work. In the evening we went to the son's house to tea. We found the house splendid, the husband is an engineer gone on business to London. We returned to our inn and made ourselves comfortable with whisky toddy which I found agree with me remarkable. I hope to have some in Swanage.

Thursday 26 March: We took a general survey today of all the Quarries. We found the stone very badly manufactured, men earning 45/- per week and some more than this. The consequence is the alehouse gets the money in place of the poor wife. We dined with Mr Johnson after this journey, who had a lovely wife and a fine family of children. We had a good dinner and a hearty welcome. We returned to our inn early, packed up and went to bed, not forgetting our toddy and absent friends.

The next morning — thus we finished our business in Aberdeen. It is a fine city. Union street is a very elegant street, the fronts of all the houses is faced with granite finely dressed. The statue of the Duke of Gordon in granite is beautifully executed — I think far preferable to King William the Fourth in London. Then there is a Banking House nearly opposite with granite Corinthian capitals, what I had never seen before. The marble and granite works of McDonald and Leslie (got the contract for two red granite fountains for Trafalgar Square) was far above anything of the sort I have ever seen — columns 18 ft. long, polished in great perfection. The Scotch may well be proud of their skill.

Friday 27 March: Friday morning, 7 a.m. We are now off by the *Defiance* Coach for the south. We came on to Dundee where we dined. The day was beautifully fine and though we paid inside fare we gave the outside preference. When at this inn, I discovered the two inside passengers were Mr John Hunter and son who once resided in Grosvenor Place. We did not know each other in consequence of his unskilfulness towards me when very ill. We arrived at Edinburgh about 7 o'clock p.m. after a pleasant day. We now were anxious to find our way to Newcastle but to our great mortification all the night coaches were full. We had only one chance left us and that was two inside places by the Mail through Carlisle, from thence to Lancaster where we arrived in the evening having travelled all night and all day. We had just time to get dinner, when we got into a first-class carriage and the next morning we were safe in London having travelled from Aberdeen without stopping, except for a few hours in Edinburgh.

BACK HOME IN SWANAGE

Monday 27 April 1846: This morning I commenced opening a ground for a cesspool in the garden for a new water-closet. Charles and Henry are at work for me. We found the beer-cellar covered with clay and rock at the back of the cellars. The men were working until 10 p.m.

Tuesday 28 April: This morning I have been to see Miss Cole's house with Mr Smedmore and I advised to take away his men who were stripping the roof, the east and north walls being out of upright and the rafters are rotten and the strength of the roof is lost by the tie-beam being cut off to give head-room. The ends of the principals are also rotten and there are strong proofs of the dry rot having made its appearance. I see no other chance than taking it down for it might fall into the street and kill those who reside opposite. The roof will force out the walls, being heavy and covered with stone. It would take each floor down with it.

We are going on well today in the garden. There were 8 vessels loading here today, people must be getting lots of money but there is as many poor as ever. Last night the contracts were decided for St Clement's for 3 years. I hope we were successful. This I cannot know until Thursday, when the Metropolis will be decided.

Wednesday 29 April: This day the Metropolis contracts are decided. Tomorrow I may know. I have been all day in the garden with Henry and Charles Mowlem taking out earth and stone for the new water-closet. One of Burt's boats sunk with paving, Robert hard at work,

Edith ill upstairs, Mrs Burt in London, Mr Burt in the Isle of Wight, or somewhere else, Susy Burt in the shop (what is this to me).

▷ Henry and Charles Mowlem are brother Robert's boys. Edith Miller had married Robert (jr.) Burt, and it seems as though they continued to live at No.1. Susy Burt — what, if anything, is to be made of this aside, except that we know that J.M. "loved her from childhood"?

Thursday 30 April: No good news from London today. The Wizard is in the field again, he is a bad fellow and all his friends are bad. The day has been fine but the evening is rather gloomy.

Friday 1 May: Good news from London. I find we have 10,000 yards of granite to Metropolis Roads Office. Thank God for this! I went on the shore, walked for a long time, wrote Captain Fowler also Mr Robert Johnson of Aberdeen and ordered 20 gallons of whisky of the best quality.

SUMMER INTERLUDE

One of the most delightful mornings I have ever seen, the sea is like a mirror, not an air of wind, birds singing, the cuckoo also with her welcome two notes. There are 12 vessels in the Bay, not a ripple to move them.

I walked to the Fort as the sun went down, The day continued fine and the sun set beautifully. Six a.m. a very fine morning not an air of wind, the sea as smooth as glass, the fields as green as an emerald and all nature is enchanting. The birds are singing, the sea-bird floating on the bosom of the ocean appearing to say "Who so happy as I". The sea is as clear as crystal — I never saw it more transparent. About 2 p.m. there came on a very thick fog.

The fog of yesterday is gone. We had a little rain through the night. The wind increased as the day advanced and at 2 p.m. it blew very hard.

Five a.m. Washed, shaved and dressed before six o'clock. This is a beautiful morning, scarce a breeze, the sun is shining rather faintly, the sea smooth.

Whit Tuesday. Wind ESE very moderate and the people all alive. A beautiful day and all appear to be happy. An omnibus going to Adam's house and back with boys and girls at one penny per head, also boats plied at the Quay for a trip out to the vessels for one penny for each person. Dancing in the old fashion is going on with great spirit at the White Hart.

It has been very hot today. The thermometer in the sun was one hundred. There has not been a breeze today; the market boat left in the morning and is now come back; she has been under Ballard Hill all the day. So has the *Gertrude* cutter. She has been in the same place. The sea is as even as the face of a mirror. The winds of heaven are hushed and all nature appears happy, the fields are green, the birds are singing and the sky beautifully blue. There is a poor boy I hear, who fell over the cliff near Worth. He fell into the water and was drowned. If he had been taught to swim he might have saved his life; this day is gone and one more fine never was seen.

This morning is like the preceding, not a ripple on the face of the sea, the market boat has had another start for Poole but to no purpose – not a breath to fill the sails. Men are obliged to tow their vessels into and from the loading-berth. The sun is again setting in a beautiful manner, the curtain of night is once more drawn over the lovely face of nature. May my life close thus calmly.

Another morning the same as yesterday, the thermometer at 80 in the shade. Morgan's boys all went to bathe today, this is the 2nd time this week. My namesake is frightened, he is badly taught. Still, he is a sharp fellow.

▷ "My namesake" was Henry Hibbs's and Sarah (Manwell) Mowlem's boy, born 1840. It seems that he was in Morgan's school.

Another such beautiful morning as the preceding, the barometer at a stand-still. The cuckoo is delighted today and all nature seems refreshed. There is scarce a wave on the shore. There are a few clouds to be seen but which course they steer I cannot tell. Since I began this there is a breeze from the south but I suppose it will die away, it will be burnt by the sun.

A little small rain, which will refresh the earth, the vessels are now able to move. Last week passed away with scarce a breath of wind.

There are 4 vessels in the Bay, the water very smooth, the sky a tinge of reddish pink. The night that has passed has been very hot, the tide is up. Fog is hanging about the hill but all will be heat, though there is a few drops of fine rain.

8 p.m. Mackerel sky. There are 30 vessels here, wind being west, the ebb tide being gone they are all brought up for the next ebb. The evening is most serene. As I was sitting with my wife and watching the sun sinking behind the hill I heard very distinctly a deep rumbling noise, it was too sharp for thunder. It was the sun-set gun at Portsmouth. This is a great distance.

I have been working in the garden until the perspiration ran off my face. The gardener Hatchard was inebriate or drunk.

I had a treat yesterday. The captain of the Coastguard, Captain

Grandy, took me in the cutter *Gertrude* to Kimmeridge. It blew a fine breeze SW and we had an ebb tide. We went through St Alban's race inside and I never been in a heavier sea, she dipped in both ends. I really thought she would wash us off deck. All stood fast and it was a magnificent sight.

Up before 6 o'clock, the day fine. Everything now proclaims the summer, the corn fields look more and more prolific. The grass, the corn and all the fields appear as though Providence will be bountiful to us this year. The idea of famine is to me, dreadful. May God avert this.

I was up this morning at 4 o'clock, saw the sun rise. This day, 53 years ago, Earl Howe fought his brave battle and was the cause of sending numbers into an unknown world. God hasten the day when there will be no War. The morning is as fine as ever it was when first the world was made. When at dinner, a whirlwind came and blew our glass door on the staircase to, and smashed three large squares of glass to atoms. I went aboard a Billy-boy [a one-masted trading barge] the *Excellent* of Goole. I was anxious he should go to Guernsey for stone but he was a stranger to that coast.

This morning the Queen of England had arranged to start from Osborne House to Scotland, round Land's End, but the morning is foggy. The Queen passed Swanage about 11 a.m., but the fog was so thick she could not be seen.

DOWN TO EARTH AGAIN: THE WATER-CLOSET

May 1846: Had my nephews taking rubbish from the garden with their horse until 8 o'clock p.m. My bricklayer is moving on a little faster. 6 a.m. My bricklayer was here at 4 o'clock this morning and is getting on well with our little job. We have the old closet down now, therefore not convenient for the inmates. All the clay is removed from the grass plot. I paid my brother 30/- for moving away rubbish from my garden, two sons, one man and a horse for two days work. My cistern is fixed, it is of lead and will hold [?] gallons of water.

TO LONDON AGAIN, THEN TO GUERNSEY

Thursday 14 May 1846: This day I am going to London. My return will be soon as I enjoy health here in great perfection. I must leave my water-closet job in the charge of Mr Smedmore. I am going to meet the Blackfriars Bridge Committee tomorrow respecting the repairs of the Bridge which was finished by me five years last August. It has worn well and is now in good repair to what some of the carriageways are in London.

I arrived safe in London by half past 8 p.m., being gone by rail in 2½ hours [Southampton-Nine Elms] for the sum of 10/-. I met the Committee and after a little the contract for the repairs was given to me − I saw there was a good feeling in my favour. I promised Mr Montague we would soon complete those repairs without stopping the traffic.

I left London by the 3 o'clock train for Guernsey via Southampton. Went aboard the *South-Western* steamer, Capt. Goodridge, Senior, and after a passage of eleven hours we were safe in Guernsey Roads. I landed and called up Mr and Mrs Burley who was well and glad to see me. I remained in the house the whole of the day, the wind was SE and it blew strong. I was glad to rest.

Monday 18 May: Hired a horse and gig or a chaise and drove to St Sampson's with young Burley. Saw le Maitre and numbered about 24 vessels in the harbour. As it was blowing very hard S by E and the rain heavy, I did not proceed to the Quarry as I intended but sent for all the men to meet me after work at St Sampson's. I drove back to Mr Burley's to dinner, and at 6 o'clock I was again at St Sampson's. There I saw a great number of the men and thus addressed them: "Men! I have served you many times and oft. I have crossed the Channel in gales of wind to meet you and pay your demands. I have never deceived you neither have I ever asked you one favour. I am now going to ask you to make a few thin cubes for Blackfriars Bridge. I cannot control you but I ask this as a favour − one hundred tons will be enough, it is not much more than a ton for each man, and I should like them in a fortnight. When this order is completed I shall, if I live, take up the list and carefully look through the names and see who are my friends." This was a hard hit to those who did not intend to serve me. On this I left them with a kind Goodnight.

Tuesday 19 May: I intended to leave Guernsey this day but it was blowing very hard and as I had several little things to do, I put off my journey. I called on Blanche, she was looking very well but I fear she will never obtain the high position she held with me and my wife. All this was pointed out to her before she left our house, she seemed to understand. I called at Mr Randell's, whose house is still full of children. In the evening I went to the Assembly Rooms to hear a Mr Bumball, a phrenologist, lecture on education and am willing to confess I never was more delighted, but few indeed were auditors. It is true he had given lectures before.

Thursday 21 May: The weather more fine, left Guernsey at 12 midday with the *Monarch*, Captain Richard White; came through the Swinge with a strong wind, heavy roll of sea, arrived safe at Southampton at 1 a.m., 22nd, left by the Mail train at 2 o'clock, arrived at Paddington at 6 o'clock safe and well. I remained at the Wharf and my lodgings all day.

Wednesday 27 May: Went to Epsom races with Mr George and Joseph Nicholls, Mr Browse, two Cadogans, R.K.Burstall, Murray Anderson, G. Burt and J. Freeman. We were all merry but the day was hot and the road very dusty.

Saturday 30 May: Left London by the 7 o'clock train for Southampton, then proceeded by the *Emerald* coach to Wareham, then to Swanage. Once more arrived safe, thank God. I have this day received 22 gallons from the Huntly Distillery, Aberdeen, for which I have sent a cheque, cash included, £17.11.0.

PLUMBING AGAIN

My men working at the new water-closet will, I fear, exhaust my patience. Men do more in one day in London than any man I have seen in 3 days here. We have moved all packing-cases out of the beer cellar and cleaned up a bit in the garden.

Our new cistern is full this morning for the first time. We shall now have a good supply of water for the closet, and to wash hands in the lobby. The carpenter is putting on the locks. There is some chance now of finishing this little job, which has taken twice the time I intended.

▷   Quite soon he is busy with more improvements:

I have some workmen here cleaning drains and preparing for a bathroom, which will be a great comfort in a house.

I have this day received my new copper bath and shower from Keeps, of Chandos St., St Martin's, London. I hope I shall have many real comforts from this bath when I have it fixed.

The men are come to fix my bath.

Busy all day fixing copper bath.

Used my bath for the first time this morning, it was warm and comfortable but not like warm baths in Ems or Wiesbaden in Germany. Those are too delightful ever to be forgotten.

June 17 1846: I am off to London today to consult about Mason's work for the Office of Works. [A note in the margin:] Safe return July 11 ... Succeeded in getting Mason's work for the Queen.

TO FRANCE

Left London via Southampton for Guernsey by the *Lady de Saumarez*, Captain James Goodridge, Jr., commander. I arrived in Guernsey at 9 a.m. on July 1st, after a rough passage, wind SW and strong. I went to St Sampson's in a carriage with Mr and Mrs Burley and saw le Maitre and found all correct there. Remained in Guernsey until Friday, 3rd instant, learnt that Blanche was married to a Mr Hugo. I then left Guernsey by the *South-Western* Steam Packet, Capt. Goodridge, arrived in Jersey at half past 9 a.m. Saw Mr Thompson respecting the French granite which I was anxious to know all particulars of and where it was to be found. I left at 11 a.m. the same morning for St Malo by the *Princess Royal* Steamer, arrived in St Malo about ½ past 4 o'clock, saw John Ferguson who was there for his daughter who had been to school. I am glad to find a person that I could tell what I required. A man looks a great fool in a country when he cannot speak a single word of the language. However, we dined at the Hotel de la Paix, Maillard, St Malo, and however Englishmen may complain of dinners in France, I found they knew well what was good, for I enjoyed myself very much. The wine was first rate and as it was the first day of Dog-days, I found it very agreeable to my thirsty soul and I did rejoice that I was not a teetotaller.

I left St Malo at ½ past 9 a.m. full inside after 12 o'clock at night. Not one word could I say to my companions but when daylight came all had a jolly gaze at me and seemed to say, such as you whacked our country-men on the plains of Waterloo. A fine-looking Frenchman with a long beard and eyes like ferrets looked as though he would like to make a hole through my body. He had a young wife with him but he stunk like a pole-cat. I did pity the wife and despised the man.

I arrived at a very pretty town on a hill called Avranche. You get to the top by a zig-zag road; the country all around is full of woods; you can see the sea. I never saw so pretty a town and if ever it rains it must be clean. I was there before 5 o'clock a.m. on the 4th and had to remain for another diligence to take me to Grandville, so I had an opportunity of seeing the town which I did. I found the Chapels open and looked into these, all therein appeared devout. Here, for the first time in my life, I saw our Saviour on the Cross as large as life, very high, and nailed. This gave my feelings a shock for the moment.

At 6 o'clock a.m. there came my other diligence for Grandville, where I arrived at about 10 o'clock. There were a great number of females beating clothes in a stream of dirty water. On leaving the diligence a very pretty girl addressed me in English and recommended me to her hotel. I said, "I hope it is respectable". She answered "Yes, as any in the town". So I think it was. I took my breakfast and was a little refreshed after travelling 76 miles without eating or drinking. The little bedroom I was shown to − the floor was as dirty as the street, not a bit of soap or any water. After this I said, now for Choisey, the Island of Granite [Ile Chausey], how am I to make the French understand what I require? After asking several if they spoke English, I saw a packet from Jersey. Now, says I, I shall find an Englishman or one that can answer my purpose. So I did, and got a man to arrange for a boats crew to row me to the island. I then, through this man, found out a Mr William Reeks who was engaged on this Island for the French Government to build a large lighthouse. This was lucky.

I started with my French crew and young Mr Reeks who was kind enough to accompany me there and back. I found in place of one Island, fifty-two islands, that are never covered with the sea. The granite is beautiful and like the best Aberdeen. It is, as it were, growing out of the mighty deep and in very large blocks, not a single bit of earth on some of these islands. The Quarry-men appear to move about from place to place where the stone may easily be moved. There is a good harbour and, though open, there are little islands that check the sea from being heavy in this little place formed by nature for the protection of man. I found about 400 men at work dressing granite for Paris streets and bridges and harbours.

Having had a good survey we started back and it took the men 3½ hours. Just before we landed the wind sprang up against us. We arrived at 10 o'clock. I took my dinner at my inn with young Mr Reeks; at 12 o'clock I laid down on my bed but was called at half past twelve to go on board the *Princess Alexandria* bound to Jersey. I got safe on board then I had to exhibit my passport and then I found I had neglected to have it visaed. Had it not been for the kindness of Capt. le Seller I should have gone back for 3 or 4 days but he gave me a hint that the fellow was poor and I gave him a bribe. At the moment we were about to start there was an order from the shore to hold on. Now, thinks I, I am booked! On board came another boat and the first that was asked for his passport was a crusty old Englishman. He said in England that he had produced it once and he would see them damned before he would show it again. Whilst this was going on we were hanging on a single rope and the vessel appeared mad as the breeze was strong and fair, the Captain singing out "Are you ready, Sir", the vessel was cast the right way and the troublesome Frenchman stepped into the boat. Off she flew like a bird on the wing.

Sunday morning in Jersey harbour. The morning was beautiful, the sea smooth. As we arrived here the *South-Western* was moving her paddles to move into the Roads. I said to Mr John Goodridge, "Stop her a moment", which he kindly did, and on board I stepped, glad enough to be free. I had a good wash on deck and after that a good breakfast. At 8 a.m. we started with the Mail on board for England. The morning was beautifully fine, wind SE, but before 9 o'clock a.m. the wind veered to SW and began to freshen, the sky thundered and there came on a very heavy thunderstorm with lightning, hail and rain; the sea was very rough. It was awfully grand. We got safe into Guernsey roads. We went on at a splendid rate, yards and topmast down, reefed sails, and we went through the Attack Passage, and we were from that rock the Attack, to the Needles rocks, in 5½ hours. I never travelled so fast. We arrived at Southampton Docks about ½ past 9 p.m. I remained in my berth until one o'clock a.m. July 6th, when I started by the two o'clock train for London where I arrived safe at ¼ past five having travelled more than one hundred miles per day. I slept two nights in Guernsey, otherwise I never undressed until my return to London. I was thus 3 nights without taking off my clothes. I am much pleased with my journey and have written to Monsieur Jobert W. Guilbert, 18 á Caen and have sent to his foreman on the Island of Choisey two Aberdeen stones, one three inch cube and one four inch cube, as a pattern. I have no doubt but this will prove a good business for Mowlem and Co. under the kind protection of Providence for all I undertook to do appeared as though I was greeted by the kind hand of the Almighty. I hope my fellow men may reap the benefit of my hard exertion.

Thursday 16 July 1846: I received a letter from Captain Simon Fowler stating that the new ship is launched, she was launched the 10th instant at Hartlepool, and her measurement is 166 tons new measurement. She is to be a brig and called after me. She was launched on a Friday. May success attend her and her crew and may providence shelter her from the storm.

TO GERMANY

Thursday 23 July: At 4 a.m. We are going to Poole this morning and from thence to the Rhine for the benefit of Mrs Mowlem's health, with Susy Burt and Mrs Elliot. I shall give a rough sketch of my trip to Germany.

We stopped at the Ship, Charing Cross, from July 23rd to 26th, which cost us about five pounds. On July 26th at 10 a.m., we left London by the *Antwerpian*, Capt. Jackson; Joseph Freeman, George Burt and T. Hall accompanied us to Gravesend. The day was fine and the steamer being a fine vessel, we soon reached this place where we parted with our young friends. We were now steaming for the ocean; we paid our fare, 42/- each person; we were a goodly company; we had a good dinner but at a very high charge. We were at the Nore at 3 p.m., course SE. 4 p.m. SE by E; 5 p.m. E; 6 p.m. ESE. This takes you into the Scheldt. There is a good light at Dunkirk, also at Ostend.

We arrived at Antwerp at 6 a.m. on July 27th in 20 hours. We went to the Hotel Labourers where English is spoken, the comforts not very great to an Englishman who has a comfortable home. I asked for Mr Jones and was taken just without the door to a little place like a three-cornered cupboard or a large pepper-box or a small watch-box. The height was about 5ft.4in. and about 2 ft in the clear so that I could neither stand nor sit, and what to do with my hat I could not tell. I began to think I had got into the wrong box, but the fellow who was kind enough to show me spoke English very well. Before dinner I went to the Cathedral, it was magnificent in the extreme.

This morning I took my party to the Cathedral who were all equally delighted at the splendour. The sculpture was far, very far, before anything I have ever seen in England. I have seen the works of Flaxman and heard him lecture. I have seen Richard Westmacott, also his brother, and have often seen Chantrey and his best work. But there are about four figures in Antwerp Cathedral that are as much superior to any of the above that I fancy I could tell in a dungeon the English from the Flemish. There is a tameness with the English, whilst with the Flemish there is a sort of living fire about them. We took a survey of St Jacques Cathedral; this is not so large as the other but if possible it is more chaste. The white and black marble, and the masterly hand that has prepared it, is very far better executed than any masonry that I have ever seen. The long screen with ¾ columns and the rail and base − the close joints would make an English mason blush unless he was lost to every manly feeling.

I strolled back to the great Cathedral where I could pass months. There is constantly something new to be seen, some fine points of masonry or some new line which you had overlooked before. The Cathedral is not exactly E and W but in order to show you this there is a fine line of brass sunk into the black marble floor and it is so neatly done that I wondered what it was, for it was like a hair line. I was informed by one who is stationed there, "It is," said he, "the meridian, Sir." So by this I found the Cathedral was E quarter and SW quarter

N. It struck me as there is a variation in the compass since this was built, or it was laid down by the compass in place of taking the meridian at noon?

The Tower is as the great warrior describes it, like fine lace. How a man could deliberately direct his cannon against such a place of art, and how he could sleep after taking away paintings and robbing the House of God, I cannot conceive. All those things, when he had time to reflect on a large, barren rock (where I still think he ought to have been) — his conscience must have weighed very heavy with him. In Reubens Square there is a cannon ball left in the front of one of the houses for the rising generation, I suppose, to look on and reflect that there was such a man as Bonaparte that did his best to destroy that beautiful city.

I was very pleased with the market for vegetables, it was immediately opposite our hotel. It commenced early in the morning and by 10 o'clock every basket was gone, every cabbage leaf was cleared away, not a vestige to be seen, not a market woman with her Flemish bonnet and wooden shoes.

Thursday 30 July: We left Antwerp a little after 9 a.m. in a first-class railway carriage. We passed on to Mechlin where we exchanged carriages. There was a great bustle and confusion. I was not sure we should not be taken back again or on to Ostend or Paris. I now began to feel the want of two or three other languages. We then went on to Tulement, Liege, Aix-la-Chapelle and Cologne where we arrived at half past 8 p.m. I never was more fatigued and the weather was hotter than ever. We were obliged to open the windows in order to breathe; we were then smothered in clouds of dust. When we did arrive at the station at Cologne my troubles came on more thick. I got the ladies sent off in a cab to the Rhine Hotel, then it fell to my lot to look after the luggage which, thank God, was not much. We were all packed into a small, square room, the porters in a dock with a dwarf wall to keep off the passengers, every package has a number and the owner has another number of the same sort but then how could I tell when the fellow called mine? When the room got a little more quiet I thought as money spoke all tongues, I would have recourse to it at once. I caught the eye of a fellow that appeared as though it was a longish time since he had a tuck-out, and slipped some silver into his hand. It was well managed by both. Still, I saw the fellow was frightened, but not at me. I showed him my number, he soon had my bags on the dwarf wall and asked his superior to feel but be did not and I walked off with my all. I find if I had been caught giving the man money, I should have been taken care of by the police. I got into an omnibus and went to the

Rhine Hotel. I thought I should melt in the omnibus. There was an earthquake at this very moment when we were on the move to our new lodgings. This hard days work knocked up my wife and friends.

The smell of Cologne is just like night-soil baked in an oven. We went to bed but there was little sleep. The rooms were hot, the blankets baked hotter than I ever met with, the curtains, though beautiful and thin, was hot. I fancied everything would choke me. After we got to bed there was a fellow going past your window with something like a little Chinese drum, with two strings with a nob at the end of each string, and by giving a quick turn the strings struck both ends of the drum but it had an unearthly sound and put me in mind of Old Nick. The fellow said something when he beat his drum and I fancied it was to tell the thief to get out of the way, the father to take care of his *daughter* and also to see that his wife is in the house and if she be alone. I thought, after all, it was rather good.

Friday 31 July: I rose early and little refreshed. My first view was the noble river Rhine which is worth much trouble to get a sight of. The bridge of boats was the first I had ever seen and I was much delighted with the Cathedral, this is the best arranged cathedral I have heard in the world, it is 500 ft. long and 300 ft. wide. It will take 50 years to finish, it has been standing still for some hundreds of years but it will now be finished, for the King of Prussia doubles all subscriptions, large or small. We dined at the table d'hote, a large room but not full, some from England, some from God knows where. We went to bed in good time and we heard the fellow with his drum.

Saturday 1 August: Up to breakfast, as hot as ever. After paying our bill we embarked on board the *Elizabeth* steam packet, a fine vessel, and we then proceeded up the Rhine as far as Coblenz, where we arrived at 7 o'clock p.m., and put up to the Bellevue, a large and handsome inn full of people. We had a bed here next the street, close to the end of the bridge, where there was chattering and bells ringing all the blessed night. This is a fine place and more of a warlike town than Cologne. We, after taking our breakfast, August 2nd, booked a carriage to Ems. We dined at the English Hotel, Becker, there was a large party at the table d'hote, some of all nations. This place meets the views of my wife and her sister, so here we make up our minds to remain and try the effect of the waters. Susy Burt and I proceeded back to Coblenz and the same day slept there. The next morning we took a survey of the town and bought some dresses, a cap, I know not what besides. After all this we took an omnibus to Ems where we arrived in time for dinner with our new dresses for each.

I forgot to name, at peep of day, just under my window, about 20 men came with picks and shovels to dig a trench for gas or water, and the talk — I could fancy Irish and my own men!

Monday August 3: I rose with the sun and made up my mind to sketch the great citadel, Ehrenbertstein, which is exactly opposite the hotel Bellevue, but to my great mortification I found the fog had shrouded nearly the whole of it. I have never seen such a fortification, it will contain 100,000 men, all my country-men run over the bridge of boats and hurry up the hill as though they had not a moment to live. I was content to look at the outline — I fancy all the inside — but God help an enemy that may ever take shelter in Coblenz, this great citadel would shatter down every house in a few hours, Napoleon would have found his work to do here.

When we arrived at Ems per omnibus we agreed for apartments with Mr Becker at the Four Towers, a large house, high rooms, standing in a fine garden bounded by the River Lahn. We had two rooms, second floor, at 4/8d per day. We had servants to pay besides this which made it come high. Mrs Mowlem had her dinner brought from the hotel every day; Mrs Elliot, Susy and I went to the Hotel d'Angleterre, Becker, where we had in the very hot weather to spin out an hour and a half. There was chit-chat, yavo, and stuff-stuff; my goodness how some of them did eat, and not a dish of any sort but what they partook of. I would rather take some bread under a hedge alone than be obliged to dine at a foreign table d'hote. It is well to see and mix now and then, it gives you new ideas, but as for comfort! At a place like Ems the great go to see and be seen. There is the Marquis of Duro with Lord and Lady so-and-so, and Colonel and Lady so-and-so. Then comes a Captain in Guards, another in the Blues, and Lady and Miss who-knows-who; this party looks down on everybody unless they happen to be a relation of some of the above aristocracy. Then comes the relations of the great Rothschild who are Jews but they cannot help themselves. Then come the O'Briens from Paddy-land that *would* be in spite of fate a relative of some aristocratic personage that has just left the hotel.

Yet all this lot dine at 1/8 for a dinner, no wine but water! Then up goes the eye-glass, then the glass of water, then fall back in the chair, then another quiz with the eye-glass, "Oh, dear me, who is that vulgar person there? I declare they are English! I declare they never ought to have left the plough! Oh, I shall by-all-that-is-good-and-great, expire! Pray, my dear Lady so-and-so, do you happen to know who that tall, ugly fellow is, with three dumpy women, who came without any luggage?" Another quiz. "I daresay, dear, they come out of some Union House or Penitentiary."

"Oh, ha! ha! Good, I declare!" Another look. "Why, they are at the Four Towers! Poor Becker will never get his money, you may depend!"

Tuesday 4 August: I rose at 6 a.m. and went to the spring and like another, took of the waters; dined at the table d'hote with about 100 persons. I found from sad experience it would be impolite not to sit an hour and a half or two hours at dinner, and though I had nothing else to do it was a bore for me. Well, I said, I am here for the health of my wife and I must make the best of it; the world was not made for me and me alone.

I have taken a fancy to Seltzer water.

Saturday 15 August: Morning. I have had little sleep last night. The "pon honours" have had a dance in the house we live in. They had clubbed together and danced nearly all night. Now I think this, with due submission to high honour, that it was a great piece of impudence. Supposing a case, that Mrs Duro had been unwell, as was the case with my wife, and we common people had had a flare-up, what would have been said and done. Why, we should have had notice to quit and Becker would have been marked for life *for keeping a bad house*. But these fellows could pull Lady so-and-so about and make her *cry out and shout* and all goes for nothing and I and my family obliged to put up with it. It made me savage and I thought then that we were the only respectable people in the Four Towers. I could only compare this dance to one in Wapping or Portsmouth Point and I am sure their conduct was as bad as any on Tower Hill.

Mrs Mowlem with her donkey-man makes the most of her time, we drink water, take three meals per day. I take it easy as my legs are not able to carry me very far.

Took my delicious bath which is one of the greatest comforts in life. I remain always 30 to 40 minutes. My usual time of rising is about 6 o'clock. I manage to hear the Opening Chorale.

Heard the beautiful Chorale.

Sunday 23 August: Walked in the Kursaal with Mrs Elliot and Susy Burt. The gambling was going on at two large tables. The dancing commenced in good earnest and all was well conducted as if at a place of worship. The band was fine in the extreme and the dancing was very fine but this was Sunday and God forbid that I or any other Englishman should fall into this error and forget the greatest blessing of this our English home − the Sunday.

Saturday 29 August: Thank God this morning has arrived. We left Ems at 7 o'clock. No man was more delighted that I was to leave this place. I set my back to Ems, and never had the curiosity to look behind me. I believe we were all glad to get away; it is true we thought well of the Kesselbrunnen waters, for we were improved, but as for anything or anybody else, we cared not. No, not even for Lady O'Brien , nor Miss Ferguson, or any of the Miss Bulmers. We shall remember "fling" some of them would give at meeting. I can only compare this fashionable movement to a vessel head to wind when she is pitching head and stem, or the duck when he dips his head under and then his tail or stern, bustle and all. However I am at all times disposed to be very respectful to upper ranks, I do hate all this, the slow manner of speaking, the forced hysterical laugh which is keyed nearly at the bottom of her wind-pipe.

Well, we travelled with a nice pair of horses and a very neat carriage. We passed the old castle of Nassau on the right. There is a chain bridge over the Lahn here. The castle is a fine old ruin and no-one can pass this place without calling back some of the delights and also the suffering that all these places could record if the young virgin and mother were allowed to come back, when the gay are merry-making under the very battlements where crime of the deepest dye has been perpetrated. But all is hushed in Death; all is still as the grave. But there is a drawback when you look on these heaps of solid masonry, the small trap-door, the entrance some 15 feet above the ground where the ladder is drawn up at night, where the deep well is within, and the assassin's bloody hand uplifted. There was no one then to tell the tale, the deeds of darkness was done and who could tell, now there is nothing but the bloody spot from which we are all at liberty to draw our conclusions ... and to thank God we live in these enlightened days. We arrived in the City of Wiesbaden about 5 o'clock at the de la Rose, the landlord spoke English, we had two bedrooms and one sitting room.

Sunday 30 August: We dined at the table d'hote at one o'clock for the first time in this place. I did not much like it. There were some English shop-keepers that appeared to look on you, as you had just arrived, as if you had no right there. The dinner was good and we had left off water and bathing in some degree and took once more a little wine which we all needed. As we did not like the table d'hote we agreed to have our meals in our private apartments. We went to the Kursaal and the gardens. The building is one of great splendour, the marble columns and caps are of beautiful workmanship, the sculpture excellent indeed, the chandeliers of the most costly description, the floors in diamond shape laid with close joints and very neat. The room is open for all classes, but every man, rich or poor, must take off his hat as though in a place of worship. There you may take your place at the gambling tables, and under the same roof you may have your dinner and your coffee. You can stake your cash at the table and not say a word, some lost their money without any apparent trouble or pain, and others, I could see, felt the smart most severely. I kept mine in my pocket. It is not very pleasant to be cheated at your hotel but it is far worse to be done at the gambling table. We were delighted with the gardens, the dashing ladies, the all-nations, the beautiful shrubs, the flowers, the walks, the trees, the shade, the sunshine, the swans, the ducks, the water, and all that can be to make this life happy. Then there is the band of about 30 performers who all play so correctly that it is like one instrument. All this for nothing. Some of this band play as they did at Ems at 7 o'clock a.m. and they begin the day with an opening chorale of very slow movement and it is solemn indeed. It is calculated to make a man forgive his enemy. I wish we had something of this in England; but in spite of this prayer, there is the gaming-table, the dance, the anything. The Sunday is forgotten. We were all as bad as the rest. We went to our hotel, took tea and coffee and went to bed early, glad to rest from Sabbath-breaking.

I have been this morning to hear the band at the celebrated hot spring, that which is described as salt chicken broth! About three o'clock this afternoon we heard heavy peals of thunder in the distance. It came nearer and nearer. Then the rain came, the hail such as Handel speaks of – it ran along the ground – the lightning flashed, the thunder rolled along in deep note and all was sublime. The evening was fine, the moon shone forth in all her glory. There was a thick cloud about SSE and the moon E. The sky was clear except this cloud and it had the appearance of a large citadel where there were some persons on every side discharging fireworks. These flashes were every moment. You could not tell from what point they would come, but so it was, and it was one of the most sublime things I have ever seen. We were obliged to leave it to the hand that made it. We went to bed begging protection from that almighty hand.

This evening I took Susy Burt to the theatre to see and hear the opera of Masoinello. I had heard this more than once in London but I never heard it so well executed before. We had a place in the second tier boxes and paid 2/- each.

▷ The opera would have been Auber's *La Muette de Portici,* first seen in London at Drury Lane Theatre in 1829, when it was better known as *Masaniello,* after its fisherman hero.

We are all on the mend. We are living better although the servants were all charged on the bill. I thought a little bribery might improve our table so I gave the waiter and also the cook something for themselves. Our table cut another appearance. We had lots and lots that was of the very best kind, and a great abundance as well. We lived jolly indeed. It is here as I suppose it is all the world over, bribery and corruption, nothing done without. We were much pleased and as we were paying a high price we thought it no sin to live for our English money. We had by this time found out a wine we were much pleased with. We found a bottle, rather small, it is called Marcobrunner, it was not strong but there was something in it that made you [on] remarkable good terms with yourself.

This day I with my ladies have been to Schlangenbad about one and a half hours from Wiesbaden. This large bath house is built in a narrow valley or rather between two high hills with woods, where there are, from appearance, lots of snakes. It is a place for billing and cooing. It is reported serpents often secrete themselves in your bath and entwine round your legs whilst in the bath. The bath-house stretches or strides across the deep ravine and how in the first place a man could think of building such a place, and in the second place how he could conceive that people would go there to spend their money (and they *do* so) is one of the most extraordinary things I have met with. It is true my eyes are not yet open, nor never will be now, in this strange world. The great Rich and Wise could answer the above questions, I shall never visit this Schlangenbad again and if I had not I should have cared but little, but this, with other strange sights, has done good to my wife, therefore I am well paid for my trouble. We passed through lots of little villages of most singular construction.

This day after dinner, took our carriages again and drove to the Platte, the shooting box of the Duke of Nassau. It is about 1300 ft. above the Rhine, it is surrounded with very thick woods and full of game and lots of stags. The house has 4 fronts, plain and good, the entrance right and left has two of the most beautiful stags in bronze I have ever seen. We went inside and saw the different rooms which was rich indeed. I saw a little box to spit in in every room, bedroom like the rest. The beds were very nice, all for one person. The floors were all of walnut, very clean and very slippery. There was the Green Room, the Red Room, etc. The house is very much exposed but each window has shutters of sheet iron that folds back on each side, and being painted look very pretty. In the centre of the house is a round well-hole, the top lights the whole of it, as you enter there are two stone stair cases beautifully executed. It would puzzle a mason to know how they are fixed. They are both left handed and I was inclined almost to believe that the place was built to suit the stone staircases. They both rose and finished at the same level. I could not discover any joints. The dome is in sunk panels with trusses projecting and on each truss there was placed a buck's head and horns. This looked very singular but was all in good keeping for a shooting-box. I hope some day to make such a plan. The door jambs were all of polished marble and the doors sheet-iron. It would stand a good hammering if an attack was ever made. A huntsman here must be bold indeed; I saw in the rooms more than one bear's head. I saw a young man with a double-barrel gun and not only that but a sword as well — one that would cut down a tree! The fellow was dressed as snug as possible and by his shoes he was in what I should call full practice. He was munching an apple after dinner. He had a dog as strong as a donkey and his mind was made up for business. We were all satisfied with what we had seen and we remounted our carriage to return. The apple-trees are all open to the highway, no fence, no hedges, no walls; but the laws are such that no man would dare to rob another. The great Duke of Nassau would cut them up like pork.

This day we made another start by railway to Frankfurt to see all we could see. We dined at the Roman Emperor for one florin each and a pint bottle of good wine included. There was an excellent dinner, lots of company. We got back to our hotel in Wiesbaden in good time but with rather less cash than we started with. I got decoyed in my old age into a dashing shop and was eased of £23.13.2., besides dinner and travelling expenses. This was our farthest trip up the Rhine. There are some good sights to be seen but let any man bring with him from Frankfurt three ladies to London, and let him know only as much English as I know of German, and if he does not look a sam, my name is not John, and he will go home if he can without seeing much. I went to my bankers here for cash and got it.

This day I went to Mayance to hear the Prussian Band which excels if possible, all I have heard. I really felt for the poor fellows — the passages some of them had to perform made me feel for them. There must be severe measures taken to get this done; the master of the Band looked daggers at them. There were thousands of people, some taking coffee, some wine, some ices. All appeared to have plenty of money and see who could excel in dress.

Walked from the town SE on high ground. There is a very old castle on the summit of this hill. There are some short, stumpy shrubs growing round this old place of sin, for I look on all as such where deeds of darkness have been committed. I had a long look at it and saw there was no door below, but an opening about 10 ft. from the ground. This put me in mind of the Eddystone Lighthouse. This was at the height to keep poor souls in or to prevent those outside from coming in. These reflections were sad and sorrowful and they made me sad. As the sun just dipped its face below the horizon there came a large bird with long, lanky wings and legs a little drooped and made two or three circuits round this castle and down he settled, fearless of me. Is this really a bird or is it the ghost of some poor, murdered, innocent virgin that had suffered there, or was it a guardian angel to watch over the ashes of some beloved friend, husband, lover or wife? As the darkness advanced I left full of thought.

I thought my brother Bob may throw some light on this as he believes in ghosts and hobgoblins.

I bathed today in the Hotel Rose. The bath was like a two-stall stable, partitioned off with boards about 7 ft. high. So if you are disposed to have a look at your neighbour in the next stall, you may do so. There is a peep-hole in your door with a bit of wood dropped over it. The man therefore has an opportunity of taking a view of any person he pleases. He was a fine young man that had the charge of the baths. He shuts the door and it is locked to the bathers. There was room in my stall for two to bathe — mine was a two-stall. When the man was mixing the scum which was on the water I said, "Do two bathe here at the same time.?" as there were two rough baths made of coarse brick. He said, "Yes, oh yes, very often. It is for two persons." Then in the floor above there are lots of air holes about a foot square — or peep holes. I did not care for myself, but I could fancy some of these German fellows could talk about some of the great folks of England. But I have heard ladies are not so particular from home. Look at Ramsgate, look at Margate, look at Brighton, take a look at Swanage shore in summer-time with your glass if you have the slightest curiosity. Some that bathe there in their own town or village look as demure as an old whore at a christening, but after going by railway about 50 miles they throw off those modest looks and their conduct makes some who indulge sometimes in rather a rough joke, blush for their ragged or open bathing dress.

This is in my opinion in keeping with these open bathrooms I saw; but they are not all so. I suppose the open stalls pay the proprietor best, otherwise he would have them constructed on a principle where a modest woman could go without fear of being overlooked. There is not a lady in the land but would turn up her nose at this remark of mine unless her bathing-dress has at all times been tidy. I write this as my ideas strike me. They are, if I live, to refer to myself, and if they fall into other hands I care not a farthing whether the party be pleased or not. I have been there and back at my own expense, trusting I shall never want the money.

We are now about to start from Wiesbaden, bag and baggage, for old England. We leave our Rose and the respectable Mr and Mrs Schneider who have behaved very kindly to us. Of course they have made us pay, it is their business; besides, they are obliged to speak English for us, we are in consequence much indebted to them, and if we were to go there again we should go to the Rose, if Mr and Mrs Schneider lived there.

We left at 7 a.m. in a carriage and on going out of town we paid our passage by steam boat that was to start from Beherich at 8 a.m. We were there on time and the packet, a fine vessel and very clean, came alongside and took us on board. The day was fine, the tide over ebb, away we went with a goodly company. We passed Asmannhausen and Oberwesel and at Mid-day we were at Boppard. This part is beauti-fully grand, a strong tide, high hills and sharp turns. If a vessel were not quick she would be on the rocks. From this place we soon got to Coblenz. So on we went gaily down this magnificent river. Dinner time came but previously the little steward came to everyone saying in good English "Do you dine at the table d'hote today?" "Yes, with three ladies." And when the bell rang I was astonished to see such a dinner and the number of courses. I left the table thinking all had finished as I wished to see all I could. After some time my wife and party came and said there were several courses after I left. There was a fat fellow sweet on Susy Burt, and if this man did not eat and drink as much as a wash-hand basin, why ask the ladies! You may visit my house in London, lords, private or public hotels, and you don't find a dinner so good, and all this for 1/3, no stewards fee.

Your wine you pay for at a moderate rate, all iced though the weather was so hot and we were on board a steamer. Where they found the ice I know not. You had only to choose your wine from a wine-card and there was the charge fixed. At 4 o'clock we were off Bonn, where Prince Albert went to college. And we soon had the crane in sight on Cologne Cathedral, one that was fixed there some hundred years ago. And when the building of the great and beautiful tower was stopped for want of funds, this very crane was taken, so Murray says. There came on a dreadful thunder storm and such was the superstition of the inhabitants, poor as they were, they had this crane put up again, and an immense thing it is. I was looking at it with wonder and amazement when the jackdaws started from it and at that moment I saw it turn round with a change of wind without any noise. It must be beautifully constructed and the timber must be good to have remained so many years, but it will be no longer required; for if the Cathedral should ever be completed, which I have no doubt it will be, the railway scaffold will finish it for they have it there now and the mason's work is rich indeed and all appear to be working in proper order, no noise, no shouting, but every man at his post.

6 p.m. Here we are once more in Cologne. We got into a cab and were driven to the German Hotel or Hotel d'Allemagne and a very dashing place we had. We had coffee, looked about the city. I met our guide that was with me when we first arrived but as I had not shaved and had on a chamoney hat, the fellow did not know me. As the train was going to start at 6 o'clock we had to be up at 5 o'clock. The waiters were all behind, therefore we had a poor breakfast and a ride of 16 hours before us. This was no joke for an invalid. I thought if we got over this long journey we should all live for ever. Thank God we did it!

At Ostend we embarked on board the *Queen of the Belgians* and arrived at Ramsgate 10 minutes before 2 p.m. We went to Hodges Hotel, took refreshment, and left per rail to Paddington via London Bridge, where we arrived at 8 o'clock, glad indeed.

Saturday 21 November 1846: Saturday evening at half past 8 p.m. arrived in Swanage safe and sound once more, thank God!

☆　　☆　　☆　　☆　　☆　　☆

Thursday 17 December 1846: From November 21st to this day I have been very careless in not entering up each day. One reason is I have made some long memorandums of Guernsey. I hope now to be regular in my little remarks. We have the wind north, where it has been for about 18 days, with a fine wholesome breeze, a strong frost every night and very cold for poor people. I went to Weymouth the 8th instant to see Captain Fowler and to induce ships to go to Guernsey, where he is gone. I brought Miss Fowler back with me. I hired a horse and gig from Mr Rowe, cost me there and back £1.12.4. I slept at Captain Fowler's house, young Simon has a bad leg, he is obliged to remain at home. On 14th instant I went to Wareham to meet Miss Browse in a fly. It was very cold indeed. I have been much engaged in repairing two plaster figures which was broken on its passage per rail from London. It was figures of Minerva and Diana most beautifully sculpted but broken all in bits. I much regret this as it was a present from George Burt. I shall only make a botch of them.

Friday 18 December: Another sharp frost which agrees well with me. I drink a tumbler of cold water every morning and wash my body with cold water though there be ice on it. This is a treat. I have been too busy through the whole of my life to indulge in this sort of cleanliness.

I hope, while I have life, I shall be able to have this comfort. The evening is one of the most lovely I ever saw.

I have been south of this place to see a poor family, the man's name is William Gillingham, he has a wife and 4 children, he resides in a small house near a barn belonging to a man named Groves. This is an abode of poverty. The man has 8/- a week. His wife is a [?] dodle like too many in this district. I shall try to assist them.

Thursday 24 December: Lots of people here begging. We have given away lots of beef and pence to the poor. The night was cold, the singers as usual sang their Christmas carol, one of Mr Joseph Manwell's. He, poor man, had an idea he could compose music and passed a great deal of time in arranging in score. His sons were his band. He sang as well as he could, then found fault, then sang again, then altered a few notes until some of the quick passages looked as black as a thundercloud. He did his best and all his arts were moral but he was *not* a master of music.

Friday 25 December: Christmas. The morning is strong NE, frost and cold. There is a Revenue Cutter on the North Ledge with her head NW, quarter moon today, high water at 2 o'clock. It is the *Petrel* from Weymouth. She strikes heavily at high water and if the wind should increase there will be loss of life. The men ought to be allowed to leave her for, as she is in broken water, how are boats to get alongside in a gale of wind? Soper, of the *Gertrude*, with his boats crew today would have been swamped if they had not been very expert. Three or four heavy seas rose nearly at the same time and broke very heavily near them, but all was well managed. I have dined here with wife and Miss Fowler and Miss Browse, and am alone this evening, all hands being gone to No.1 and the maids to see their friends.

Saturday 26 December: The *Petrel* is off the rocks today, taken in tow by the *Gertrude* to Weymouth. So far all is well, but there was great danger of swamping the boats in broken water.

Tuesday 29 December: I have made out a list for Swanage poor to receive rice at 2d per lb. and salt fish at one penny per lb. There will be a loss on this but we pay this loss by subscription from the inhabitants. I wrote Mr Stamp asking for money out of my own pocket which is too bad of him to allow me to ask.

OFF TO GUERNSEY AGAIN

Saturday 9 January 1847: Left Swanage for Guernsey via Southampton where I arrived just in time to catch the mail packet, the *Windsor*, Captain Goodridge, Jr. The wind was SE and strong with thick weather. I never saw a night more dark. I arrived in Guernsey on the following morning, Sunday, at 5 o'clock. Went to Marshall's Hotel and went to bed for 3 or 4 hours. Dressed and went to Mr Burley's where I passed my day comfortably.

Monday 11 January: This morning I went to St Sampson's Harbour and as I was on my way I saw a brig in the Small Russel which proved to be my namesake, and the moment I got to the south quay the vessel took the ground. Le Maitre also met at the same moment. It will be a long time before the like will happen again. Neither of the three persons knew of our being about to be there. It is a very singular coincidence.

Friday 15 January: The *John Mowlem* left St Sampson's about 5 p.m. and the wind was SE by S which made it very dangerous. I hope all is well with her. Had an interview with Mr Nicholas Bracke for a piece of land next the Vale Mill but could not agree, went to Mr Hombers and so far agreed for ground with stone in it E of the Island.

Sunday 17 January: Went on board the *Windsor* mail packet. Wind E, fresh breeze and hazy, heavy sea off the Caskets. Took our departure at half past one p.m., NE ¾ E, which took us to the Needles where we saw the lights at 8 o'clock and got into smooth water. Arrived at Southampton at 10 p.m., went to the Royal Hotel, Matcham, and arrived at Swanage on Monday 18th at ½ past 7 p.m. and found all well.

Monday 25 January: Off to London with Miss Browse.

Thursday 11 February: Returned from London with a sad cold. The ground is covered with snow and the frost very severe. Many thing in London took my attention. I had an interview with Jennings respecting the Guernsey trade, arranged with Mr John Gore (the scavenger) for a piece of land opposite No.13 Wharf at £20 per annum from 10th instant, arranged for G.B. and J.F. to go to the granite quarries to meet Martin & Son. This interview will give us a command over the London market for the supply of granite. I dined with Alderman Johnson, shook hands with him, his brother, James Walker Esq., Sir James McAdam, who all dined at Willis' Rooms, King St., St James's. I was much delighted with the speeches of the evening. It was a bitter cold night with a deep snow.

Friday 12 February: I found on my arrival here my brother-in-law, Robert Burt, very ill. I fear he will die. It is an awful thing to die. The day closes with a frosty air.

Saturday 13 February: This morning has closed the life of my early companion, Mr Robert Burt, also many years my brother-in-law. His father and my father, John and Robert, were early companions. They paid the debt of nature. I, with all that I know, must also pay the same debt. The world will go on just the same as though we had not been. But it is a sad thing to die. He departed this life at 2½ this morning. This is one of the most lovely days I ever saw; all is serene and tranquil like the evening of a well spent life.

Sunday 14 February: This morning at one a.m. George Burt with his brother Robert arrived from London in consequence of the death of their father. I have not been out today, it was wet and gloomy.

Monday 15 February: The wind is WSW, blowing strong; the snow is all gone, the air is more mild. Still, all is gloom as my friend, Mr Robert Burt is at No.1, dead. All must be solemn and solemn indeed when so near our own domestic abode. I wrote H.C. Elliot, Mr Burley, Randall, Fowler, Mr Maillard and enclosed 88+88 = 176 queen's heads to pay for newspapers to be handed to some of those who read the Star a year or two ago. Honesty is and always will be the best policy. Yates who was the father of lies will find he has done wrong more than once towards me but I forgive him. I would rather be the sinned against.

Tuesday 16 February: The day disposed to be a day of spring. But there is the hand of death next door. Who can rejoice and be glad?

Wednesday 17 February: Nothing new today, all is gloom and sadness. Barometer very depressed. I have written several letters. All is melancholy, melancholy. I have not been out of the house yet, but thank God my cold is better.

Thursday 18 February: This day is dull like those that are gone before – melancholy. This day Mr Burt will be consigned to the tomb. His work is done and will be forgotten. All felt as though he had lost a friend and a brother.

▷ Robert Burt's elegant tombstone still stands [1989] in the old graveyard south of the parish church. It is a classical fluted column upon a pedestal and displays the ebbing Georgian style before the onslaught of unfortunate Victorian "medieval" design. The inscription says: "Sacred to the memory of ROBERT BURT late of Victoria Terrace in this place, stone merchant, born September 30th 1788, died February 13th 1847. He was an affectionate husband and father and for his many virtues is justly remembered by an unusually large circle of friends. Also Lettie his wife born August 16th 1786, died February 14th 1851. As a wife and mother she was exemplary."

Sunday 21 February: In the evening I went to the Methodist Chapel. Few are indeed left that went to this place of worship when first opened but still there are a few and I amongst the few. The text was "Prepare to meet thy God", preached by Mr Verco, a young man of

Robert Burt's monument (1847) in the old graveyard, photographed by David Lewer.

promise, but he has much yet to learn. He said little of my brother-in-law, and as he knew little he did right to say little.

▷ Tradition (and indeed the memorial monuments, one in the chapel) says that in 1774 Mary Burt, Robert Burt's mother, carrying her baby, walked to Salisbury with two other women to bring John Wesley to Swanage. He stayed the night at her cottage which stood just below Purbeck House. Always known as Wesley's Cottage it was badly damaged by enemy action in May 1941 and later demolished. On his second visit in 1787, Wesley preached in the Dissenting Meeting House built in 1705, rebuilt in 1837 and is now part of the United Reformed Church. The first Wesleyan Chapel, on the opposite side of the High Street, was completed in 1807. Its spacious successor was opened in 1886. The old chapel, used as a school room, was demolished in 1907 to make way for the Centenary Memorial Hall.

Monday 22 February: Walked to my brother's quarry. There was room for thankfulness. It was where my forefathers worked, but though the self-same woodbine is still there, alas, where are those who toiled there when I was a boy?

▷ From the above it seems that both the Burts and the Mowlems worked in the same quarry, if not Tilly Whim, then the only clue comes from the 1839 Swanage Tithe Map which indicates Robert Burt occupying plots on the North and South Common fields.

Tilly Whim Caves, drawn by Philip Brannon, 1859. "We were bent on a Gypsy party to Tilly Whim."

A Purbeck quarry, drawn by Philip Brannon, 1860.

Saturday 27 February: Wind E and more cold than ever, sky very cloudy and black, winter in perfection. What will the poor do? I have sent 1 cwt. of coals to old Sally Bonfield who is bad off, and also advanced William Bonfield 10/- on account of teaching boys. I have been to Knitson today for a way-rate and called to see an old woman whose house I took shelter in to avoid the press gang. I was then a mere stripling of a boy but tall, and though so young I was told if they saw me they would shop me, so I went from my home and asked for shelter in this lone house which was kindly given me. I suppose it is 46 years ago. I was allowed to lie on the floor on an empty sack; stone floor, this was my bed, and I well remember the fleas was like to devour me. I was glad when morning came and the press gang was gone. My bones ached. I went to my house as cheerful as some that had a softer bed. However, they had only humanity in giving me shelter, and today I gave the old woman a trifle for old acquaintance.

Sunday 28 February: After leaving church we came by the way of Northbrook. I went to step over a stile and fell headlong, smashed a new hat all to pieces, tore my new coat, and damaged one finger and dislocated another. I wonder I had not broken my neck. I remained at home all day, rather down.

Thursday March 25: We have improved our offices at No. 13 Wharf, having left No.8. We have made arrangements to take the whole of the Mount Sorrel stone for one year, which is a a very heavy affair. I, with Thomas Burley Esq., of Guernsey, purchased a brig for the coal and stone trade. I am to hold one third of her. She was bought for £1290. I gave a cheque on the 22nd instant for £100 to bind the bargain. She is a fine vessel, measures 213 tons old measurement, 203 new, built at Prince Edward Island. Her name is *Aliwal* and young Simon Fowler is appointed master at six pounds per month. Success to her and the brave young captain. I am chosen overseer and way-warden this day with Thos. Strickland and Mr Hopkins. I saw Lieut. Clarke an the Fort who is much the gentleman, had a long chat about sundry matters. I have sent the deaf and dumb boy Pearson to work this morning to pick the hard pebbles from the beach to break for the roads of Swanage.

Tuesday April 13: to London. Left for Guernsey, April 15th, where I remained until May 9th, having been much engaged to find out the particulars of Thomas le Maitre's system of doing business. He has been guilty of forgery for years. He was a religious man but a greater rascal I never met with; he is of course dismissed from our employ. He has lost a good friend in me. He will walk the earth and the finger of scorn will point at him. I arrived here, after being a week in London, with Mrs Burstall.

Monday May 17: Trade here very brisk, put provisions very dear, indeed bread 1/1 per loaf, but this is only about half the price it was when I was a little boy. It was then 2/-, or 4/- the gallon loaf or peck loaf.

▷ It was reported in the Poole and Dorset Herald [29 April 1847] that the potato crop in the Isle of Purbeck failed there, as elsewhere. Application, with sanction of Rev. J.L. Jackson, was made to the Earl of Eldon and Geo.

Bankes Esq., M.P. for sufficient funds to provide rice at 2d lb. and fish at 1d lb. for labourers of the parish whose wages did not exceed 12/- per week. "The lady of G. Bankes also gave large quantities of soup to the poor of Studland."

Wednesday May 19: A fine day for those who go to Epsom — a system of gambling for the higher classes. But the poor fellow must not sport his few shillings on the chance of a turn up card, *he* must not try his luck. Though no man sees gambling in a more horrid light than I, for I have never had the slightest inclination to do anything of the sort. I am sober and too fond of money to gamble.

This day our new brig *Aliwal* passed through the Small Russel to Jersey, Simon Fowler, master. She has on board 300 tons of coals. She looked well. She had all her canvas set. Yesterday I sent Mr Burley two nine-gallons of our best beer from the brewery of Swanage.

Swanage Brewery, demolished 1893. In the 18th century it was Gillingham's Malthouse, then Panton's and Strong's of Romsey Brewery.

▷ Swanage Pale Ale was renowned as the equal of Burton beer, thanks to the quality of the local spring water. At the turn of the century the brewery was known as Gillingham's Malthouse. Later it became Panton's Brewery. Hardy remembered the great fire on 8 November 1854 when the premises were entirely burnt out, only the walls standing. He says that James Panton rebuilt them at great expense, with new machinery. The brewery was closed down and demolished in 1893, soon after the opening of the railway station.

Up at half past four a.m. At 5 a.m. the London Mail is brought to Wareham by rail and to Swanage by 7 o'clock, therefore we get our letters before breakfast. This is a boon indeed for it brings London now very near. We get through Southampton without being robbed, for what with porters, waiters, etc., etc., you were nearly eaten up.

I received a letter from Mr Burley this morning in 20½ hours after the Packet left Guernsey Roads. Mr Burley wishes to charter the *Aliwal* to the Danube for corn at 20 per quarter. She would make £1500 and clear 1000 with good luck, but she is wanted in the stone trade from Guernsey as we shall require about 50,000 tons this year.

▷ It is clear that Mowlem & Co. was trading in coal as well as stone, and now Burley is turning to corn. But Mowlem thinks that granite has first priority, though one notes that wheat arrives at Falmouth and Waterford in October. Again he goes to London.

Wednesday July 7: Left London with Mrs Freeman and 3 daughters at ½ past twelve mid-day and arrived at Wareham at 5 p.m. by Express Train. Fares to Southampton £2.10.0. From Southampton to Wareham £1.0.4, fly and man, tolls etc. to Swanage 16/6, omnibus 1/6, George -/9, gates 1/6, driver 3/-. We were all fatigued enough for the rail road from Southampton is new and rough.

▷ The extension of the railway to Dorchester, known as Castleman's Corkscrew, had just been opened, but celebrations were somewhat curtailed as the Southampton tunnel had collapsed in April and was still closed, though some trains ran from Blechynden (later Southampton West Station) to Dorchester. The tunnel was eventually opened to through traffic in August. The Poole and Dorset Herald reported [3 June 1847]: "The opening of this line turned some of our old friends, the stage coaches, off the road. The *Emerald*, Southampton and Weymouth, will, in a few days, be off the road altogether. The *Union*, Southampton and Poole, performed its last journey down on Tuesday night, and up on Wednesday morning, much to the regret of the friends of its worthy proprietor and driver, Mr George Wiltshire." Subscriptions to him were progressing. It was also reported that he had been "appointed superintendant of the light goods and parcels department, but at which station is as yet undecided".

Friday July 9: I have a letter from George Burt saying Joseph Freeman was yesterday stepping out of an omnibus and was knocked down and run over at the foot of Waterloo Bridge. Much bruised and cut about the head and hands. Thank God he is no worse. I have lent Messrs. Burstall £50 today — which is to be returned.

▷ Again he goes to London "to assist Mr Freeman who has suffered from his accident by being run over by a gig". And back.

I find on my arrival Mrs Travers was dead, having fallen from a gig. Her leg was broken; amputation was the result. Her son Frederick was driving. She was the master and man of the Inn; the Bar Parlour was the Vestry Room for more than 30 years. The family was nursed therein and having been present when all the scandal of the place was discussed, both male and female must know a good deal and the latter knew much more than would sound pleasant to a husband's ear. Mr Travers has been first on all occasions; he had had to *eke* out a bit of bread to the poor, very often when he thought fit and only then. Not a soul high or low has escaped the slander of this meeting who congregate all the year round and decide on all matters, public or private. I hope any alteration will be the better for the poor. God help the poor and needy!

▷ In an advertisement [Dorset County Chronicle, April 1843] for the Ship Hotel, H. Travers, "her father and herself for 30 years" is the inn-keeper."Last summer the house was almost rebuilt and enlarged." Warm stables and lock-up coach houses were available.
In October 1847 the Ship was taken over by W.J. Furmage.

Went to church today, heard Mr Jackson preach: "Can a mother forget her suckling child?" I can say some in Swanage do. I have engaged Trakes to do little jobs in the house, water the front, etc. He would not say how much but he said a shilling or two now and then.

I have a letter from Timothy Trust (anonymous) giving Bob Fowler a sad character. I am sure he is a sad rascal and never ought to have command of the *John Mowlem*. Let a man take care of his friends, he may at all times fight his enemies.

Wednesday 18 August: I left for London via Poole, was 5½ hours going there in the Market Boat. I arrived safe and called at the Strand where there was lots of work going on. We were putting down thin cubes, 1590 yards at 19/6 per yard. All this was done in 8 days. I measured the work in the Strand and left London at 9 a.m. on August 25th and arrived in Swanage at 5 p.m. The man that drove me in a gig nearly drove over a boy in the street opposite the Dissenting Chapel.

Thursday 19 August: I went with Joseph Freeman and George Burt to Her Majesty's Theatre to hear the great and celebrated Mlle. Jenny Lind.

I find the money very scarce in London. Half the trades people and merchants must fail unless something quickly be done.

Saturday September 11: I have removed two stone posts from the front of Miss Smith's house that were on the same spot when I was a boy and has ever been an obstruction to passengers. I have widened the street to enable two waggons to pass, also removed the old curb which caused a hollow, and a most dangerous one to horse and man.

This has caused the inhabitants to open their eyes.

Working on lowering Church Hill. The stone we dug is marble rag such as the church is built with, or rather the church tower, which was built before the birth of Christ. I received my telescope from Dollands.

▷ The date of the tower has been much discussed. It was Thomas Manwell "the Swanage philosopher" who proposed its almost prehistoric age. Others suggested that the tower is at least older than Corfe Castle and was built as a defensive stronghold overlooking the former estuary and swannery. A more recent view is that it was attached in the 14th century to a 13th century church. However, until 1500 St Mary's was still only a chapel-of-ease attached to St Nicholas, Worth Matravers, and connected by the ancient Priest's Way.

Tuesday 12 October: This is my birthday. I am now 59 years old. My life is like a dream. The *Susan Godfrey* is arrived from Falmouth with corn from Ismail.

Wednesday 13 October: I am not well at all. I am laid up with a sort of erysipelas between my toes. My right foot is much swollen, I have no doubt but it is the erysipelas. I am requested not to drink beer nor wine, take pills or mercury and black draught. And something worse. Mrs Norseworthy of Oxford Terrace, Paddington, came here to dinner today with her two daughters Emma and Lucy, both first rate young ladies, a brother of 10 years whose name is George, I can say but little in his favour. The mamma is the same as ever, she was free and happy. She came in her own carriage, quite in style.

Mrs Noresworthy left us today, much pleased with her visit. My foot is better today. Mr Burley is gone to Waterford to see the *Susan Godfrey*.

My foot, thank God, is better. Mr & Mrs Wilcox are here in my Tower with Alice, looking at the moon, Mars and Saturn with his belts, through my telescope

▷ The Dorset County Chronicle commented [25 May 1848]: "The Planets. Mars is now to be seen in the south-western part of the heavens every clear evening. The beautiful planet Jupiter, to the south of Mars, and higher in the skies, will attract every person's attention. His belts and satellites afford ample amusement to those who are in possession of good telescopes."

I have this day received a letter from Mr Burley who is in Waterford, Ireland, with the *Susan Godfrey*, taking care the wheat is not delivered before the money be paid. The *Aliwal* left Guernsey on Sunday for London with stone. On Monday we had a new omnibus with 3 horses for Wareham at 8 o'clock in the morning, fare 3/6. It is in time for the 10 o'clock train. Just the thing. We have the *Velocity* and *King George* loading curb for Lambeth.

▷ There are no diary entries for November 1847, but the local newspapers supply information instead. First, at the end of October, there was an important meeting held at the Victoria Hotel concerning a proposal for an Isle of Purbeck branch railway. Some 40 people were present with Mr T. Hunt of Godlingston in the chair. Mr.T. Phippard of Wareham, a solicitor, "who is, we believe, the originator of the scheme" gave the details, including the probable cost. John Mowlem proposed: "That it is most desirable that a line of Railway be formed from Wareham to Swanage with as little delay as possible". He was a member of the committee which met on 19 November. It was reported that the survey by Capt. Moorsam was nearly completed. In December there was talk of a tramway through the stone-fields, and a pier was hinted at. But there was opposition from Wareham and landowners, and the scheme came to nothing. A further proposal for the railway in 1863 received an Act of Parliament approval but this again failed. But at least John Mowlem got the first pier and tramway built in 1859, well before his death in 1868.

Thursday 18 November: "Wareham station is to be lit by gas – one of the first. It already has the advantage of the Electric Telegraph." The first station was built east of the level crossing. The present station was opened in 1885 when the Swanage branch was at last completed.

Thursday 11 November: "Swanwich" (sic) – this was the old spelling, and it is a pity that the name was not retained. Fireworks night, and the shops closed at 6 p.m. Nearly all the male population turned out. Many fireworks were "let off" on the quay, banker land and in the streets. "The 'wild ones' did not forget to kick about the dangerous fire balls very freely. These matters are, we think, carried too far and ought not to be allowed in the town."

Friday 3 December: I am very busy carting stone for the street here, the road is so soon cut up. I find there are 1500 tons of stone taken through this narrow street with waggons with 3 and 3½ tons in each, with 3 inch wheels. This would destroy Guernsey granite. The wind is high, the rain is falling, the clouds are heavily overcast and the night is dark as a dungeon. My friend Thos. Burley is crossing the Channel tonight from Southampton for Guernsey. Mr John Bailey from Wareham has just called to say there was a horse at their house for me from London. Notice was sent from London to Wareham to say the horse would be there this day. Telegraph message: "A gentleman will be in waiting at Wareham for it. Mr Mowlem's horse will leave for Wareham by 11 o'clock train. Signed, G. Burt." It has been a very stormy night. It was a fearful night at sea.

Monday 6 December: The barometer is now as low as I have ever seen it, wind SW by W blowing a gale, the rain heavy. This is winter indeed and bad weather for the poor fellows that have to get their bread at sea. I was up at 6 to go to Wareham for my horse but the weather was too rough.

Tuesday 7 December: Up at 6 but on examining the barometer I found it more low than I ever saw it and I find the one in our counting house was nearly as low as at Paris in 1768.

Wednesday 8 December: I am off to Wareham for my horse. I rode him home. He is a fine horse, carries me well, rather gay.

Thursday 9 December: This morning I have received a letter from my friend Mr Burley who was at sea on Saturday night, also Sunday night, in the *Conscience*, Goodridge, Jr. After going out of the Needles put back to Yarmouth Roads. Then made a start and put into Portland Roads until midnight on the Sunday. Then got under weigh again in a dreadful gale, saw the Caskets at 6 Monday morning, got into Guernsey Roads at 12 mid-day after one of the most terrific passages that man ever crossed the Channel in. The hand of Providence did protect him with the gallant crew.

I have been to Kimmeridge where there is a vessel burnt to the water's edge with cotton and rice. Her masts, bowsprit and decks are all gone, nothing left but the bottom shell. She is on the rocks, head NE. I rode horse-back there met with a Mr Voss and his son, found him a very clever fellow for a Dorsetshireman. He rode first rate horse and is a gentleman. He resides at Knowle and is a farmer. I was 5 hours on horse-back and went through Knowle and Rempstone [?] back to Swanage, nearly 30 miles.

I have been as far as Little Sea today. I find no person should cross this place when the tide is high. The wind blew hard SSE, and before I got home I got wet. I like my horse and enjoy the ride much.

▷ Little Sea, between Studland and the modern Ferry, was a century ago exposed to the open sea. Now it is land-locked since the building up of the sand.

Thursday 23 December: I have been in the house all day, bottling whisky.

Saturday 1 January 1848: We have, I find, a second order from the Metropolis, about 8,000 tons as an extra supply. This is good.

Monday 10 January: A fine cod fish from London. Tomorrow morning I hope to go to Portsmouth to look at a brig with Joseph Aslett.

Monday 31 January: I have a letter from Mr Burley this morning saying that *John Weavel*, a stone-laden vessel for us in St Sampson's, caught fire in the forecastle. She was the outside ship, the wind ENE right into the harbour. The *Susan* was next and 16 more vessels loaded for us inside. The tide was flowing. The *John Weavel* was scuttled and the fleet was consequently saved from fire. It would have been a sad job for us and the Mutual was in for about £20,000.

We have from Guernsey 18 sail of large vessels with granite for the Metropolis. Tomorrow I shall be off to London for a few days as we have about [?] ships to deliver.

Tuesday 8 February: I left Swanage per coach to Wareham to meet the 10 o'clock train to London, Express. Charge £1.8.3 to London [Nine Elms]. Arrived a little after 2 p.m., went to Lett's Wharf and commenced business, went to Paddington in the evening. At Lett's Wharf all day making out tickets for granite for Waterloo Bridge and Lambeth.

Friday 25 February: Barometer very low, very heavy sea on the shore, wind SW strong, the water higher than I have ever seen it, although it is quarter moon. There must have been fearful work at sea this night.

Saturday 26 February: The wind has blown a perfect gale this night. The barometer at 9 a.m. this morning in my tower is far lower than I have ever seen it. It was within a trifle as low as it was in Paris in 1768; it was frightful indeed. A few minutes after 9 a.m. it began to ascend a little but it blew very heavy. I have never seen the sea more furious. The *Wonder*, Mail Packet on the Southampton to Guernsey station, passed over our Ledge about 4 a.m., Goodridge, Jr., master, to Studland Bay. This was her second night out, and when she hove up the sea was terrific. She fell in at daylight, lucky for her. The large steamship, the *Hindustan*, lying to in the Channel making very bad weather of it. She however followed the *Wonder* and got a pilot boat from Studland Bay, a lucky hit, this. I never saw a vessel labour more than this large ship did. The *Wonder* came into our Bay for 12 tons of coals but could only get half that quantity as there was such a heavy ground sea. She then went back to Studland Bay after landing some of the passengers that had enough of it, poor things. I was thankful I was not obliged to go; it was not so once with me.

Sunday 27 February: Morning. The *Wonder* came again into our Bay. I went on board to see my old friend Goodridge, he was weather-beaten indeed. I gave the passengers my newspapers wherein the French King has abdicated the throne of France. This was news to them. I also told the crew of a French fishing boat the news, in the best way I could, of their King.

Tuesday 29 February: I saw a ship deep in the water off our bay in the morning haul her wind for a pilot and split her main topsail all in rags.

TO GUERNSEY AGAIN – THEN LONDON

St Peter Port, Guernsey. Painting by G. Shepherd. John Mowlem often put up at Marshall's Hotel – it is now Boots the Chemist. Courtesy the Guernsey Museum and Art Gallery.

Tuesday 14 March: Returned April 4th, being three weeks from home. I left Southampton by *Courier* steamer at 7 p.m. and arrived in Guernsey the next morning at half past two. I was in bed at Marshall's Hotel by 3 a.m. This seems impossible but it is true. I took breakfast and then called on Mr Burley, took a fly and pair and went to St Sampson's. Agreed to take a quarry of Mr Hubert at 3d per ton ground rent, went to St James Church and heard an excellent sermon preached by Mr Hartery – a little affected. Agreed with the *Resolution*, King, at 6/- per ton freight also several others at 6/3 and 6/6. There were 40 sail of vessels at St Sampson's for stone, some from two to three hundred tons, and nearly all at 8/- per ton.

Last night it blew a hurricane all round the compass. The *Venus*, Ayles, sailed in the a.m. Both arrived safe in London but they must have experienced a dreadful passage. No mail packet came up from

Mowlem's Guernsey granite quarry at Baubigny, painted by Lemon H. Michael, 1883.

Jersey this day. I have have agreed with Mr Guilbert's ships at 6/6 in place of 8/-. This is a saving.

Wednesday 15 March: The *Courier*, Captain Goodridge, left Guernsey Roads at ¼ past 9 a.m. and was in Southampton a little after 5 p.m. I arrived in London at 126 Praed St. in 12 hours and 33 minutes. This is my quickest passage. This was once an excellent passage from Southampton to Guernsey and nobody ever grumbled.

Went to the Wharf.

Went to Newbury and ordered two new barges, 310 each, guards and all complete, the *Letitia* barge to be repaired. I then went to Tollington Park and passed the night, also Sunday.

Went to Limehouse with Mr Anderson and sleep at his house in the evening.

Dined with Burstall and son at Corby's.

Dined at Praed St. and at the Wharf all day looking into accounts with J. Freeman.

Dined at Corby's with the surveyors.

At 13 Wharf with Freeman all day.

Went to the new church at the end of Star St., with Mr and Mrs Freeman and little Sue.

At the Wharf all day. Left London.

Monday 10 April: This is the day for the Chartists to meet on Kennington Common and from thence to go in a body to present their petition to the House of Commons. The Government said no, we will not allow you to do so, which they did not. The Chartists was in consequence obliged to go home having made great fools of themselves. The day is stormy with heavy rain, which would cool them.

This is a fine day. Susy Burt and I have ridden over the hill by Corfe and Kingston home; and on our return here, by Golly, her horse fell, shot her off, broke the crupper and split her habit on the shoulders. She escaped without further harm; how very lucky, as the horse was going fast. It was one I borrowed.

Tuesday 18 April: I have commenced this day to make myself acquainted with all the bearings of the Metropolis contracts which are to be delivered on 3rd May. We are connected with a party who has but little honour, though they like many others profess to be very good Christians. The price of granite will have to be much lower than heretofore. Received a letter from Mr Burley saying that *Juliana* had sunk off Guernsey, 280 tons, NE of the Heyap Rocks, crew saved.

Saturday 6 May: Left London this morning. We got our share about 10,000 for the supply to the Metropolis. We have a mail packet from

Bell Street, Herston, photographed by B.J.K. Rives.

Poole twice a week to Guernsey, Jersey and France, one of the packets belonging to the South-Western Company.

Friday 12 May: This morning I rose ¼ 3, washed, shaved and took a boat to go from Poole to Guernsey. I safely got on board about 4½. The water was smooth and the day was beautiful. We arrived in Guernsey Roads 20 minutes after 10 a.m. Our course from Durlston Head to the Caskets [Casquets] was on a full ebb, SW by S. We shaved the Caskets a little. Our course then was SW by S¼S, a beautiful passage, a fine boat, and Captain Smith a very fine young man, gentlemanly. Lewis was the First Mate. I landed, dined with Mr Burley and in the afternoon we had a carriage and drove to St Sampson's and to the NW part of the Island. I left Guernsey again by the *Atalanta*, Capt. James Goodridge, Snr.

This day I have been to church and heard a very pretty and good sermon from Mr Groom, Genesis, Chapter V v.29 – one of the most kind and pleasing subjects that could be delivered: "And the Dove returned to the ark and Noah took him in." We sin and fly back to the ark of God and he kindly takes us in.

LODGINGS AT BLANDFORD

Went with Susy Burt to Wareham outside of the coach, from thence to Blandford in a gig for lodgings for my poor wife who is very unwell. Returned at 7 p.m. by the *Enterprise*.

▷ It was reported [Poole and Dorset Herald, 2 December 1847] that the *Enterprise* coach had commenced running Swanage-Kingston-Corfe-Wareham. Proprietors: J. Bailey & Son and J. Wignall (formerly well-known whip of the *Emerald* coach, Southampton-Weymouth).

I am going to Blandford with my wife and family for her health. Arrived safe at Blandford. Mrs Wheeler's, Salisbury St., my wife bore the journey well. Now stowed away safe at an inland town.

Monday 22 May: Left Blandford at 2 p.m. with a new dog-cart, £18, lamps £2, harness £6, to run backward and forward to Swanage. I arrived in 4 hours.

Arrived at Blandford. Walked out with Susy Burt among the fields and lanes. Nothing new in this dull town. Give me London or the seaside. I remained in this inland town until Tuesday June 6th, when I went to London, and on the Wednesday I appeared before the Committee of St Martin's Parish respecting some expenses they had been at with two of our men who had stolen old stone from the parish, wishing us to pay a portion of those expenses which I refused to do, but gave them a cheque for £20 for the Parochial School.

Friday 23 June: In Swanage. This morning I saw the sun rise – what a sight for mortals to behold! The hand that made it was divine. Whilst looking at this noble sight I saw the Guernsey steamer cross this Bay of ours from Poole, how noble she dashed through the waves. Heard a sermon from Mr Morgan, such a poor sermon on predestination. I could handle a steam engine about the same as he handled this beautiful subject.

We have had an inquest here today on the body of Charlotte Keats who has been ill-used by her husband who is a young bad man, grandson of Old Keats who was a sad and wicked man. The verdict was from natural causes. Her body was opened. She lived and died in the house where my wife's uncle Thomas lived when I was a boy. This Mr Thomas Manwell was a good man and a philosopher, fond of his wife. The Coroner gave a good lecture on drunkenness. The gun at the Fort, 32-pounder, was fired for the first time today.

Wednesday 26 July: I have sent 5 guineas to the Sick Hospital, having received a letter from the Duke of Cambridge in his own handwriting – so much for Royalty. This day I have had a narrow escape of my life. I was at the Fort on horseback. The beast, that I never liked, did all he could to come home. At last, finding I was master, rose high on his hind feet and was nearly backward. I dropped off full backward, the fool came nearly on me, but I kept him away placing both feet on his haunches. The moment his fore-feet came to the ground he let fly and one of them hit me fair in the fleshy part of the thigh. He looked frightened. I mounted him and rode him home for the last time. He is a vicious beast, but though the fall was heavy I am not much the worse. I am obliged to wear my right arm in a sling.

My arm is bad. Mr Freeman has ridden my horse to Poole and back by way of drilling for misconduct.

My arm still painful. I have been to Weymouth. Drove my dog cart and the vicious horse to Wareham, then on by rail and coach. Went on board the *John Mowlem* who has put into Weymouth leaky, stone-laden from Guernsey. I have sent the horse to London per rail. I was glad to say good-bye to him. The beast cost 2.8.6. Thank God the animal did not send me into an unknown world. This evening my friend Mr Backer from London came with George Burt to see me. I have known him for 33 or more years. He is a good man and I am proud of him.

Miss Bassett married Lieut. Toby today. He thinks a great deal of himself, she a poor tender plant. Money brings great suffering on the delicate generation that such a pair will bring into the world. I have written a long letter to George Elliot, wishing him to remain in Auckland.

Thursday 24 August: This day I have sent my portrait with that of my wife to George Elliot to Auckland, New Zealand, by the *Duke of Portland* which will leave London on September 1st. Both are carefully packed. The case is 3-3½ x 2-7 and 4 inches thick, weight 37 lbs.

▷ There are at least two other portraits of John Mowlem. One hangs in the Firm's board room at Westgate House, Brentford. It was painted by R.R. Reinangle, R.A. J.M's date of birth is incorrect, showing 1789-1868. The second portrait hangs in the Tithe Barn Museum and Art Centre, Swanage, on permanent loan from relations of the Arbon family (Susy Burt married James Arbon and inherited the portrait).

Thursday 31 August: I am off to Poole for Guernsey. My friend Thomas Burley was waiting for me on the pierhead. Went to St Sampson's after breakfast, bought two quarries, paid £750 for one, size about 6 English acres; the other £145; another on lease for 5 years for £45. I gave Guilbert John a clock for the Methodist Chapel at St Sampson's. I returned by the same packet.

September 1848: People are all alive here in forming a regatta with sundry other things for amusement. Mr Jackson the Rector is much against it, he looks very shy at me as I am Treasurer. He thinks the money all wasted in vanity, poor man.

▷ Waterloo Station was opened in 1848, extended from the original terminus at Nine Elms.

Waterloo Station, 1848, from '150 years of the L&SWR', courtesy of Kevin Robertson and Amber Graphics.

Left London by the 11 o'clock train with fireworks for our regatta, about £10 worth. We had a fine day, quite a holiday. There is a regatta with boats, greasy bowsprit, duck hunt. Sailing and rowing commence with a good will, the Poole people carried off the prize. There was a duck hunt or rather 4 men in a long-boat and one in a little boat, there was upsetting the duck, 3 men in the water at once but not Swanage men. All this finished with 4 stone-lighters being rowed by two men each. William Butler who is 70 years old was the first boat, his brother George the next boat. Then began the fire works soon after dusk, first from the *Gertrude*, then from the shore under the care of your humble servant, which went off very well. All were pleased. Mr Jackson, poor stupid man, had a fling at our fun. He thinks hiself a god. But my God is far above him and I am glad I am not obliged to bow to an earthly god; it is to Him that the Universe, and all that therein is, to whom I bow.

Monday 2 October: This day we have received a new piano from Broadwoods, 95 pounds, for Susy Burt for her good conduct. I have been with George Smith to Mr Serrell for a summons for A. Keates for breaking into his house on Sunday last. This is the fellow who behaved so cruel to his wife.

Saturday 14 October: This day I have finished a good flight of steps to the trough at Court to my *own* satisfaction.[A joke at the expense of his London contracts which always ended with "to the entire satisfaction of the surveyor".] It is now free from the filth of every description, and children yet unborn will rejoice when they drink the waters. It is strange indeed that 60 years have gone by without a single improvement in this place, and God Almighty has spared my life to improve the place where I first drew breath.

▷ Dr Home's report of 1872 on the sanitary conditions in Swanage said: "Another pond (at Court) in the course of the stream, locally called 'the Lake', furnishes water for some of the inhabitants; it is much less foul than the Mill Pond, but it cannot be used after floods. At Herston, where fever is so common ... the best water people have is from a dip well, within 10 feet of the surface road drain, down which the drainage flows from the houses above ..." A well in Court Hill is marked on the Ordnance Survey map of 1886. This area is now built over, but the rivulet still emerges and flows alongside Court Road to join the Swanage brook.

Thursday 26 October: This evening I have safely returned from London, having been to Newbury to examine the new barge *Alice* and the repairs of the *Letitia*. Since I left, my much esteemed and good friend Mr Thomas Burley is dead. How awful is that word. Poor man,

The Mill Pond. Gas first came in 1868, so the lamp-post is not earlier. But, as in John Mowlem's day, there is no wall round the pond, as there is today.

The trough or 'Lake' at Carrants Court (Court Hill), improved by John Mowlem.

in the midst of life, he departed whilst in conversation with Mrs Burley at 6½ p.m., October 21st. He died in a moment, a blood vessel giving way in the heart. I have been adding some new bins to my wine

The old Wesleyan Chapel, replaced in 1907 by the Centenary Hall. The new chapel had been built in 1886. Photographed by T.J. Dibben.

cellar to stow away my Marcobrunner from Coblenz, 6 dozen in good order. Robert Burt dismissed from the Parish of Lambeth from being foreman. Misconduct.

▷ Presumably this is George Burt's younger brother. His name does not appear in the Swanage 1851 census.

Friday 3 November: My wife has another birthday, she was born in 1788. Her two sisters dined with us today, Mrs Burt and Mrs Elliot. We had some of my Marcobrunner. Mr White has discharged 40 or 50 men, not one I should say has been provident to provide for a day ahead. This will be a hard winter for them. This was a fine day up to mid-day. I could see from Durlston Head, Hurst Castle and lighthouse, Egypt Point and the lane D [a course prescribed for ocean steamers] of Calshot Castle going up Southampton Water. I gave this spot the preference to the church which is frousty, dusty, dirty, and not ventilated scarcely once in a week. And this is the Rector who has been kind enough to go from house to house to caution people to be clean. The cholera is now making its appearance in England May we escape that dreadful scourge. The brig *John Mowlem*, Robt. Fowler, master, has anchored in Swanage Bay. I have sent the crew 2 gallons of beer on board. She is a handsome vessel, her colours are flying.

Wednesday 8 November: I am now off to Guernsey. On my arrival at Southampton I found the old *Atalanta* with about 75 tons of goods on board bound at midnight for Guernsey. The night was calm, the moon shone and all looked well but it was November and the distance great, the boat old and slow, and I no chicken. I had therefore a good mind to go on shore but I took courage and off we glided at midnight, soft and slow. The moon went to bed at 3 a.m. The rain fell at 6 a.m. The wind sprung up from NNE at 7 a.m. and blew strong. This was fair. We soon saw Alderney and then the Caskets. The wind increased, the sea roared and ran high but on we tumbled and safely arrived in St Peter's in 12 hours. This was delightful, for had the wind gone to the South we should have been 48 hours or perhaps a week. I was glad to see Mrs Burley who was much better than I expected after the loss of her husband. I then went in a carriage alongside the *Aliwal* and discharged young Simon Fowler who has had command of this vessel for 20 months. I put him into this vessel and I have found him a sad rascal, unworthy of any patronage. I left Guernsey and arrived at Southampton the same evening, passed the remainder of my time in London. Saw Mr James Walker, the Government Engineer. Got an order for 5000 tons of Guernsey stone for Dover. Got the contract for Bow, about a mile of Guernsey 4 inch cubes at 11/9 per yard. The

The mouth of the Brook. See the tragedy of 29 December 1848. The cottages were on the site of the Parade.

stone for Dover 9/4 per ton, and the first time we ever gave a tender for this article.

Monday 4 December: Blowing a whole gale.

Tuesday 5 December: This morning I saw off Old Harry the steamer *Courier*, Capt. James Goodridge, master. She stood across Swanage Bay but on clearing the land the sea was so high she bore up for our Bay. The Commander came on shore with Captain R.T. Taylor, R.N., a very clever person. These two gentlemen and Lieut. Kitchen dined here with me at 1 p.m. who were much pleased with each other. I have often wished to acknowledge the kindness I have received at the hands of young Captain Goodridge and now I have caught him. The packet left our Bay about midnight. I have heard today from Guernsey that as the *Susan* was in Yarmouth Roads at anchor, the *Albion* ran into her and sunk. The *Susan* was not damaged.

Thursday 29 December: Last night the wind veered to SE to E to NE, the rain fell in torrents. Several vessels in the Bay and a collier, the *Velocity*. All the vessels went for Studland Bay except the collier. She went to sea and carried away two jibs. All the others got into Studland Bay, one went on shore, another carried away her bowsprit. They must have had a sad night of it. It was high water about 11 p.m. The sea was very heavy on the shore and this keep back all the water inland, and after 3 hours ebb-tide such was the rush of water by the brook that it undermined the foundation of a house in the occupation of Mr John Soper, master of the cutter *Gertrude*, that the front fell into the brook and Mrs Soper fell with it. She was found on the shore nearly opposite our house. She got out of bed and fell into the river and was washed and carried into the sea. Such was the force that the brook was made from about 6 ft wide to 30 ft and upwards, but the foundations was very defective and this caused the death of the poor woman. Two daughters was in the same house and two lodgers, females, and with great difficulty all were rescued by James Pushman and others.

Herston House, photographed by the Royal Commission on Historical Monuments. Here his wife died and John Ernest Mowlem, his great-nephew, was born (1868). Demolished 1967.

Herston House — "We have fixed a slate cistern and formed a dog-kennel underneath."
Demolished 1967. Photographed by David Lewer.

HERSTON HOUSE

Monday 1 January 1849: I take possession of Mr Cochrane's house and garden today for £185, also a small paddock at the east end of the garden where when I was a lad I began to whistle for my wife who was sometimes at this house with her relatives. Little did I think the maid and the property would be mine in 1849.

▷ This was Herston House, on the west side of Newton Manor which was the ancient family seat of the Cockram family. The Rev Brune Cockram, D.D., was Rector of Swanage [1614-67] and survived the Rebellion apparently without disturbance. W.M. Hardy well remembered working at the family vault when a boy when the last of the Cockrams in the neighbourhood was interred in September 1847. Herston House was unoccupied and derelict in 1967 when it was demolished. It was redeveloped with a row of indifferent dwellings. All that remains is a stone set into the back of the garden wall in the High Street, bearing the legend "J.M. 1850".

Tuesday 2 January: Wind ENE. Heavy sea in the Bay. The *Velocity* riding with two anchors, pitching heavily. In the night, about 7 o'clock, the schooner *Velocity* of Poole with about 25 tons of coals, parted from her anchors and came on shore north of the brook. The coastguard fired 3 rockets but without effect. As the tide was on the ebb it was of no consequence. She was boarded from the shore by the coastguard and a warp brought on shore. I got a little wet for I was anxious to save life, but all was safe. I went home thankful I was not obliged to go to sea. Joseph Freeman has paid into my private account £940 cash and debited me with George Burt's bill for his father's house £1060 bearing five per cent interest per annum, making £2000.

I have been cutting the trees in Mr Cochrane's house and garden until I am wet to the skin. It is a bold beginning. May I live to see it in good order. Some very heavy guns firing in the offing. It was on this day about 60 years ago an East Indian was lost near Wind Spit. The *Velocity* schooner is still on the shore but she is upright and all her coals are discharged, crew safe but must have suffered from cold and rain.

▷ It was on 6 January 1786 that the *Halsewell* was dashed to pieces on the treacherous Purbeck rocks, between Winspit and Seacombe, with the loss of 168 lives.

Saturday 6 January: The *Velocity* schooner is off the shore today. She struck very hard before she was afloat. I find a schooner, the *Gulf of Parma*, Weeks, master, with a cargo of curb for us from Mr Burt got on shore between Christchurch and Hurst and is totally lost. This is a loss of £40. Thank God the crew is safe.

Sunday January 21. The brig *John Mowlem* is now sailing across Swanage Bay with Henry Mowlem's son John Mowlem on board, bound for Guernsey to school at my expense. Her flag was flying. I hoisted mine and Mr Anderson and I went on Durlston Head to watch the brig. She came near to the Point. I could hear her canvas rattle. I am planting trees in my new garden, trees of all sorts. The fruit will be gathered in when I am dead, who knows by whom.

▷ Some twenty years later, after J.M.'s death, Kate Arbon, Susy's daughter, used to sit in the tower at Victoria Terrace, watching for her brothers coming home from school by sailing-ship from Guernsey.

Monday 5 February: I am again going to Guernsey. I returned to my home, March 20. I had a good passage from Southampton by the *Wonder* with my old friend Goodridge. I remained at my poor friend Mr Burley's house until 17 March. I was fully engaged on our new freehold on Beacon Hill in moving rubbish to find or make a quarry. I had from 20 to 30 men, three to five teams at work every day. I moved an immense quantity of stone, dirt and rubbish in the time. I had my dinner there every day in the cold. I rode there in a carriage and pair every morning and the same took me from my work every evening. On 28th February the wind blew a heavy gale and the rain fell fast, but every man remained at his post, until half past 4 p.m. there came on tremendous showers that all were obliged to leave. I never stood out in worse weather but I carried my point. I got more done by the same number of men than I ever before saw in such a short space of time. I expended about £100 but I think well spent. I paid everybody every shilling. I left on March 19 on board the *Despatch*, Captain Babot. We came through the Swinge although the weather was rather thick. We made Christchurch Head before we made the Needles.

Saturday 12 May: This morning I have been to Hurston House with Mr Smedmore to take dimensions for sundry little jobs as my wife wishes to return there, thinking a change of air will do her good.

I have been to church, what a poor sermon Mr Morgan preached all about gold in America. What has this to do with teaching people the way to heaven?

Monday 14 May: I am off to London for a few days. My brother Robert is gone to Wimborne for medical advice, he is gone by water. I gave him another sovereign. He is a poor fellow to get through this world. I went before the Committee of St Margaret's for a 1000 due

John Mowlem's stone at Herston House, photographed by David Lewer.

last Xmas. I was received very politely. I dined that day with the Cadogans. I first saw Mrs Cadogan who has lost her husband, poor man; he was 67 and a good friend of mine.

Saturday 19 May: Came home. Off to Hurston to repair the house where I once whistled for my wife. I take my dinner there today for the first time, without chair or table. It is an old comfortable house where my wife's aunt and uncle had many happy days together.

Still at Hurston House with men and an old woman, I busy chopping wood to burn, had a ton of coals delivered.

A fine day at Hurston House chopping wood and looking after the men. The drawing room is papered and looks very pretty, a man killing the weeds in the garden. My brother Robert came to see me, ill in health, no pluck, dirty and anything but that which he ought to be. I gave my coat off my back in order to hide his dreadful rupture. I fancy he will never work again.

Friday 25 May: The whole of the day at Hurston House, having things put in order, the pump repaired, which has been made above one hundred years. There are several comfortable arrangements in this old house and no doubt many a heart has been joyous therein. My wife's uncle Martin Cole resided in this house at Hurston. He was a captain in the Navy. The house was his daughter's, Mrs Sarah Cole, who married John Cochrane, Esq. We have fixed a slate cistern to hold the rain water and formed a dog-kennel underneath.

▷ These remained until 1967 when a photograph was taken of them.

Sunday 3 June: Yesterday my brother went to Blandford to consult a Mr Lee, a physician. He told him, as I have told him, unless very careful he will die, and advised him to go to a hospital in London. This he does not like to do. He is far from any idea of improving himself; he will, I fear, die without using the means of taking care of himself.

Monday 4 June: This day we go to our house at Hurston to reside. Last night we slept at Hurston for the first time. The night was very hot, therefore I slept little, my wife slept better, Miss Randell so-so. My garden is looking remarkably well. My brother Robert is gone to London today. He has now to learn how to know himself.

Wednesday 6 June: There is a letter from my brother Robert from St Thomas's Hospital. He is much depressed in spirits. He adds his case is a bad one. I wish him safe through the trouble. Mr Freeman [William Freeman the stone-merchant of Millbank, whom he met in Aberdeen] has returned from Guernsey and has written me a very unbecoming letter which I have replied to and must admit there is something I cannot comprehend in the tone of his letter, but I have no doubt it will come to light.

Another fine day. My brother down on his luck at the hospital. I am having a screen put to the house at Hurston with battlements of stone.

▷ The "battlements" appear in the photograph of the house. These crenellations now [1989] form a path to a house facing Swanage shore.

Tuesday 12 June: Men at Hurston House fixing battlements. My brother in St Thomas's Hospital has cancer in his abdomen, I fancy from sad neglect on his part − partly ruptured. I consider his life thrown away, also his son Frank.

Monday 18 June: I am going to London to see my brother Robert who is very ill indeed, poor fellow. He is his own enemy, obstinate to a degree − a man that might have been well off indeed.

Went to St Thomas's Hospital to see my brother. I found him sitting by the side of his bed with his coat off like a Swanage man. He looked pale and had begun to reckon it was all over with him, from neglect. The medical men found it would be impossible to perform an operation on him. I gave him some cash and he would leave hospital the next day and never see London again. I was at 138 Wharf all day going into accounts with J. Freeman until 4 p.m. when I left and dined with the Company of Glass Sellers at the King's Head, Poultry, as one of the assistants. I was much delighted with the party, dined well and left at ¼ 9 o'clock sober as a judge.

Saturday 23 June: Left London this day with Susy Burt and John Mowlem Burt for Swanage. [George Burt's baby son, later Sir John Mowlem Burt (1845-1918)]

Monday 25 June: This day Matthew Gillingham takes his station with us as manservant. I fear his health is not good but he is a steady fellow, wages [?], a suit of clothes and washing. Rather out of sorts, must take medicine and go to bed is a fine comfort for anyone of my name, "pig-like".

Better today, took a blue pill and black draught.

Thursday June 28: We have had a dance on the green at Hurston. Captain Pilkington and Lady called, Mr and Mrs Wilcox also came in. We had an Italian boy to play, Mrs St Hill, baby and servant came, also Ellen Manwell. We finished up with supper. I dined at Swanage and had a lobster.

▷ Captain Edward Pilkington R.N. had been appointed District Inspector of Coastguards in 1847. In the 1851 census he and his wife, five daughters and one son, were living at Osborne House, Seymer Road with a groom, cook, nurse, undernurse and two housemaids.

I paid Delamotte 40/- for my brother Robert who will never be able to work again, and allowed Henry Mowlem's wife 2/- per week to clean the house for him. Having some outer blinds hung by Trenchard to Hurston House.

▷ Henry Digby Cotes Delamotte, doctor and surgeon, of old Purbeck House before George Burt bought it, died in 1874 aged 77. His son, Dr George Cotes Delamotte who continued the practice, died in 1922.

Wednesday 11 July: Mr Cole here to dinner with all his old stories retold a thousand and three times, poor man he will never *know himself*. George Burt taken very ill for a few hours with a sort of cholera. I shot a rook flying, distance 66 yards on level, the bird was about 20 yards high. A good shot for a green hand. There is a steamer with 180 people from the Isle of Wight. Saw my brother Robert who is very poorly but he does not appear to think so much of his situation as I do, for his disease will hurry him into his grave. How thoughtless he is and ever will be so; no care — no, not one single idea.

Friday 20 July: Tomorrow I hope to go to London and arrange about some granite paving in the New Road [Euston Road].

Saturday 28 July: Returned from London. I went to Dover with George Burt to look at the new breakwater carried on by Lee and Son. It is now about 300 ft into the sea and it has to be taken 800 ft into the sea for the sum of £200,000. Not a bad price, I think. We did not tender for the work in the New Road.

Friday 17 August: The brig *John Mowlem* off the Bay, looking very handsome. She has been on the mud off Lymington at high water, and remained there for some days. There is some schooners in the Bay bound W, and 16 fore-and-aft vessels. My brother Robert is still very unwell but he goes to Chapel and sits on the stairs. Why not stay at home or go into the fields to pray? To be priest-ridden or not to have a mind of one's own is bad indeed. He has written me a letter anything but respectable. I think I have been his best friend, which he appears to have forgotten He has neglected his family in education that their manners and conduct is no better than a common navvy. Had he done his duty I could have pushed them on in life, and now they are all slaves. The *Sygnet* was stone-laden, bound W with Toms, owner. Going over the Ledge she stuck on the N Ledge and then filled. The night was dark but very calm. This was a bad look out indeed. The vessel is his own.

▷ This year there had been a bad outbreak of cholera in England.

September: I am safe returned. I am grateful to the Almighty for His kind care of me in the midst of disease and danger. I left Guernsey

Monday morning and arrived by the *Despatch*. When I arrived at St Sampson's I found the cholera ranging in its worst forms. There had died in Opie Buildings, close where I once lived and where, or very near where I lodged now — from these few houses — say twelve, there were one hundred and fifty-two people turned out of them, taken away to the Vale Castle and the NW of the Island. I was there, and there on business, but not very happy when death was showering his darts on all sides of me, not sparing the young, some of all ages went in a few hours and were numbered with the dead in the churchyard until the last day.

Since I arrived in England I find Thomas Brooke, pilot, is dead from cholera. He was in conversation with me a long time, a few days before I left. One of the most awful thing I met with in St Sampson's was a woman large in the family way who was alive at 10 o'clock a.m. when I passed her door, and when I passed again at 6 p.m. she was in her grave. This quite made me shudder.

Strong wind and rain. Very heavy wind SE. I hope this will purify the air that the inhabitants of this earth may be in health and free from fear of sudden death.

▷ In Wareham "Friday is appointed to be held as a day of general humiliation and prayer in the Town and throughout the Isle of Purbeck, thankful that we have been so mercifully preserved from the awful ravages of the prevailing epidemic."
On 14 November in Swanage "All business was suspended here, and shops closed. The church was opened for divine service both morning and evening, and was attended by large congregations. The Rev J.L. Jackson addressed the congregation — 'And be ye thankful.' The chapels were also well filled."

Tuesday 18 September: I hear my brother is still very poorly but he is very shy of me whenever I go to his house he is sure to be absent. He has made a sad mistake through life. He is vexed I sent his grandson to Guernsey to school. He said no kind parent would part with a child so young, and hundreds in Swanage said the same. We had a dust about this but he will live and die a bigot.

At Hurston all day, propping up the south front.

Wednesday 26 September: Off to London. I was up this morning at 4½ to meet Mr R.V. Burstall in the Strand, Charing Cross, to measure new carriageway paving and footpath which we accomplished a little after 8 o'clock. The amount was from two to three thousand pounds, it is a great improvement for the public, a better piece I have never seen.

Tuesday 2 October: Returned. I found my wife at Hurston House.

Thursday 25 October: I have begun the new wing of Hurston House, taken out the foundations and made the trench with concrete. My wife is very poorly. Mr & Mrs Freeman is coming to see her aunt Mowlem, this is a very kind act of hers. Yesterday I received a letter from Mr H.C. Elliot, anything but what it ought to be. I call it a very impudent letter. He has had his feet under my table very nearly 30 years or more and because I would not advance him one, two or three thousand pounds to make his fortune in a few years, and because I wrote lightly of the speculations, he gives vent to his feelings, which I care nothing about. Poor, stuck-up people nowadays! He might as well have kept his fire to himself for he thinks more about the gentleman's honour than the gentleman thinks himself. There is an end to our correspondence for a while at any rate, and I am content. My wife is still very bad; I now despair of her being well again.

▷ H.C. Elliot is probably not connected with Mrs Elliot, Mrs Mowlem's sister, or her son George in Auckland.

I am off to London for a few days, may Providence protect me. My wife not quite so well.

At Lett's Wharf all day. I received a notice per telegraph from Poole that my wife was not so well. I therefore left by the 3 o'clock train and arrived here at ½ past ten. I found my wife very poorly but thank God she was alive. The rain fell in torrents west of Southampton.

The morning fine. Mrs Mowlem has had a poor night; she is very unwell. Alas, alas, what frail mortals we are!

My wife had passed an uncomfortable night and appears to me to be sinking. She has been all her life the picture of her father; she is now more like her mother. Her spirits are good but she suffers sadly from weakness. She has for nearly two years been fed like a baby and now she cannot even take that little, therefore something must give way.

My poor wife has had another sleepless night. She is more and more weak, though still cheerful. I have read to her today and she appears to meet her fate with great fortitude. The day is dull.

My wife has passed another bad night. She slept until midnight, then her cough came on with the fever, which continued until daylight, 10 a.m. She is a little more composed. 10 p.m. Not much better, expectoration most uncomfortable which causes great exertions. Something must be wrong in the chest or lungs; I have for years known there was something wrong there.

Mrs Mowlem has had another sleepless night, her cough is most distressing, the expectoration most unpleasant. Her spirits are good, she is composed in her mind and has no desire to see anybody except those about her. Mr Jackson has been to see her for consolation.

This morning my wife is better. She had a comfortable night.

9 p.m. I fear my wife is not so well, rather more fever, at this moment very fatigued and restless. She will take a draught which I hope will compose her.

My wife is not so well, more expectoration, consequently more weak.

Wednesday 7 November: I have left Hurston House for an hour or two today, having been every day watching my wife who is very ill. George Burt came to see us on Saturday night. A Scotch ship for Tottenham Court Road laden with cubes from N Cornwall has been lost at sea in these late gales. The loss is not ours but the inconvenience is great to our firm.

Saturday 17 November: Since the last entry I have suffered much, much more than I shall attempt to describe. My poor wife departed this life, I hope and trust for a better world, on Monday morning, November 12, at ¼ 4 a.m. It was a sad and awful thing to witness the wife of my youth die. Poor thing, her mental faculties were clear and she knew well she was about to depart for ever from this world. Her last words to me were, "Mowlem, carry me about the room, will you?" I said, "No, my dear, I cannot." "Why?" said she. "Because I shall hurt you." "Oh," she said, and appeared disappointed. "And is there not one of you can do anything for me?" I said, "What *can* we do?" She then took her handkerchief carefully and wiped her face (which was getting cold) – as carefully as she ever did in her life. Her eye then appeared to lose its brightness and her breath got more and more short until she sunk into the arms of death. I never can forget the awful scene. There were present beside myself, Susy Burt; Miss Randell from Guernsey, companion; Mrs Butler, nurse; Elizabeth and Martha the two maid-servants. Her remains were taken to Kingston Church and deposited in a vault built with brick in cement and covered in with paving below and landings above. The first coffin was a shell, the next of 5 lb. lead, the outside handsome oak with name and age, 61, on a brass plate; the name also burnt in the lead coffin. There is a vault also for me, should the Almighty think fit to take me in this part of Europe. No lady in the land could be better looked on than my wife. I returned from the grave more cheerful than I expected. I had done my duty for two years most faithfully, never having been scarce ever cheerful for the fear of what might happen, as every day and every hour I thought would be her last. But extreme care prolonged her life. She was indisposed nearly the whole time she was a wife which was 37 years.

▷ On his wife's death in 1849, John Mowlem buried her at Kingston old church, on the hilltop facing Corfe Castle, probably because there was not room in the cramped Swanage graveyard for the imposing monument which he planned, and which was to mark his own place of sepulture. However, in 1855 Swanage cemetery was opened at Northbrook, and later, his wife's remains were transferred to there from Kingston. Dying in his 80th year, John Mowlem joined Susannah beneath the curious pyramidal pile which still reminds us of the important part played by Guernsey granite in the fortunes of John Mowlem & Co.

Tuesday 20 November: Time flies; I am better, thank God, but I am not myself, though time will improve my spirits. George Burt left me this morning for London, he has been a great source of comfort to me. The weather is more fine.

Friday 23 November: I am engaged at Hurston where I am covering in my new wing, it is a very tedious operation. Slates will soon be fixed, this afternoon the rain came on and we are only half finished.

The men going on very slowly with my roof at Hurston, break nearly half the stone. I have called today on the Rev. Mr Jackson to thank him for my poor wife, he was very kind to her last severe affliction. He was very polite and very gentlemanly to me − nothing about my having taken her to Kingston Churchyard.

Monday 3 December: At Hurston House all day, Linnington painting the roof. It looks well. The poor Queen Dowager is at last gone to her long home. She died on Sunday morning just 4 weeks after my poor Susan who used to ask every morning how the Queen Dowager was, knowing here disease was the same as her own

I have been busy at Hurston House. I have fixed in the top of a brick pier a solid stone about 1' 11" square and 1' 6" thick, with battlements all round and very pretty it looks. I shall fix an iron rod with a vase on top, it will give it a very pretty effect. It has not cost me much and I am well pleased with it. It will be there for a length of time.

▷ It was still there in 1967 when the house was demolished.

I have been as usual all the day at Hurston with men at work building a battlement flue in cement, and John Coffin has been lopping the elm trees in the small meadow, cleaning out ditches, etc.

I have finished putting on the chimney pots today at Hurston. There are now 9 on the 4 chimneys, with the scullery, which makes the place appear tidy and it looks as though someone belongs to it. It will be a most comfortable house for somebody. It was a home that my poor wife was delighted with. I have been busy also lopping elm trees in the paddock, a place I will, if spared, much improve. It will be a nice home for children. It is a place I shall always reverence as long as I live. Matthew found a spring in the garden. He has gone a long way but cannot find the end of it, it is constantly overflowing. I shall turn it to an advantage when I find it. This day I have found the well at Hurston House, it is in the courtyard and it is 18 ft deep, full of very beautiful clear water, full to the brim. This is worth any money to me, being so fond of cold water.

This day I have taken down the entrance to Hurston House. I form a hall and bathroom which will be very convenient.

Tuesday 18 December: Tomorrow morning I am going to London with Susy Burt. I shall tomorrow pass my grave, also my poor Susan's, who was very often very dear to me, but is gone out of this world before me. Returned to Swanage February 7th with Susy Burt and John Mowlem Burt, being about 7 weeks and 1 day. The seven weeks that I have been in London has been very exciting to me and the death of my poor Susan in November has shook my mind much. My two amiable partners Burt and Freeman has presented me with a piece of silver plate each, of beautiful workmanship, an honour to the Queen it would be, the weight is above 200 ounces, and the most handsome vases I have ever seen in my life. The inscription on each is good. They are now on my sideboard. The presentation took place after a very excellent dinner, there were 22 to dinner, some of 35 years standing. The chairman was a King of a fellow, he came from Norwich to take the chair, I shall never forget his great kindness. I am proud of the gift and also of the company.

▷ One of these vases is still in existence and in possession of the Burt family. The Inscription reads: "My Uncle and Partner, Mr Mowlem, died at Purbeck House, Swanage, on 8th March 1868, in his 80th year. He bequeathed his residence and furniture to my sister, Mrs Arbon, who very kindly returned this Vase to me on 29th July 1868. I desire that this be handed down as an heirloom in my family to show that death was the only termination to a long period of mutual affection and regard, as well as to the partnership so happily begun in 1844."

Friday 29 March 1850: I have heard yesterday in the fog the *Sprightly*, man-of-war steamer, is on shore at St Alban's head. She was going 10 knots through the water at the time she struck.

I have a new manservant and his wife to take care of Hurston

House, came on the recommendation of Jenny Fowler of Weymouth. I hope they will be of good conduct.

TO LAND'S END

I left Swanage March 30th for London with Susy Burt and remained until April 4th. Then we with Miss Browse left Paddington by the Express Train for Plymouth. We left at 10½ a.m. and arrived at Plymouth at 5 p.m. and put up at the Royal Hotel. We went on board the *Agincourt*, man-of-war, in Devonport, after that we took the Mail and went on to Truro, 56 miles through Bodmin and St Austel. There we remained one night at another Royal Hotel. It is a large town in a valley. We had a good night's rest, then a fly to Redruth. I took a fly from Redruth to Gwennap about 2 miles to see my brother Joseph's grandchildren, two little girls named Scobie, a boy named Marrish Thos. a very fine lad, the son of Joseph's eldest daughter. He is without a father at Gwennap at school. He appears to be taken great care of. The girl Scobies are living with their grandmother. I did not see the husband but the house had ground for the floor, very small. I shall never forget the inside whilst I live. Perhaps my own comfortable house makes others appear less comfortable than they really are. We then took a fly to Penzance, a very nice place, no appearance of poverty, a good many rich from the richness of the mines. We took our dinner at the Union Hotel (Bell) and then a little walk. I find a new breakwater there which will very much improve the harbour. I should have no objection to reside there.

Sunday 7 April: Went to church, one of the most handsome in the country in my opinion. The service was performed in a most beautiful manner, better done couldn't be. This church service is the best done and Swanage is the worst, a greater contrast could not be.

▷ In 1989 the contractors E. Thomas (a subsidiary of Mowlem's) completed the reconstruction and redecoration of this fine church, St Mary's, Penzance, after fire damage. The church was built in 1835 on the site of an earlier chapel.

Monday 8 April: Another fly and to Freeman's Quarry and to the Land's End. It was blowing a gale from SSE with a little rain and a very heavy sea. I had never seen this part of the country before. The Longship lighthouse is most wisely constructed, such an awful place in a gale of wind in thick weather. Here is a granite-bound coast. We went to the Logan Rock, on the top of it, that appears such a wonder. It is said to be 75 tons but I doubt it, but after all it is a wonder. This is one of the finest spots for granite I have ever seen.

Tuesday 9 April: It blew a gale of wind, we went on to Hale and Falmouth, the sea broke over the south pier, right over all into the harbour. We dined at the Royal Hotel but before dinner I took a look at Austin's and Freeman's granite Quarries here and they are really first class. I also took a view of the blue granite that is now making such a stir in London. It really is very good and next to Guernsey far better I should say for the Parks in and about London.

Wednesday 10 April: We passed at Falmouth and a most delightful spot it is. Went to the Castle and there is a fine view of the harbour, a splendid harbour.

Thursday 11 April: We got up and started with the *Drake,* Capt Saddler,for Plymouth with a strong wind, SW, a very rough passage. I was sick to my heart; no breakfast. We arrived at Plymouth in about 5 hours. Friday we took the Express for Bristol, remained at the latter place one night.

Saturday 13 April: We took another Express for London.

Thursday 25 April: Up this morning by five, my new manservant Day up ¼ 7, this wont do, which he will find out. Susy Burt with Miss Randell left for Southampton, thence to Guernsey. I have empowered her to buy the quarry-land from McDougle; I will give it her. Miss Anne Bondell is arrived here from Guernsey, she is to instruct George Burt's children which I think will be a good thing for them all.

Tuesday 14 May: George Burt has bought his house, No. 31 Cambridge Place, Paddington, of Mr James Ponsford. Discharged Day and his wife today and have got rid of two people who will never be able to help themselves. Poverty awaits them.

Tuesday 21 May: This is Whit Tuesday. I never saw such a day for a holiday. When I was a boy how different was my views of what a merry day there was in Swanage. But now everything in the shape of fun or pleasure is looked on as a sin − a sad mistake in my opinion.

Monday 27 May: All day at Hurston House weeding and looking after men making a pebble walk by the summer-house. Just after I had written the above lines the Chief Boatman here of the Coastguards came and told me the *John Mowlem* was again on shore just inside the Needles. She has a cargo of coals for Weymouth and has just had a heavy repair at Newcastle, having been on shore at Flamborough Head with the wind free, which cost £130 to pilots, fishermen, etc., to get her off the rocks. And yesterday she must have gone on shore on a weather shore. So much for Bob Fowler, one of the greatest fools I have ever met with. And his father is telling me constantly what a first rate seaman he is I begin to hate the name.

Wednesday 29 May: At 4 p.m. I saw the John Mowlem close under the Isle of Wight with studding sails set, wind SE, nice little breeze. I hope she will arrive safe. I find on Monday 27th inst., just as she was turning out of the Needles, she ran on the rocks at Colwell Bay at 11 a.m. and got off at 11.30 p.m. after delivering 25 tons of coals to some vessel and throwing overboard 26 tons more. She got off and ran back to Yarmouth Roads. Here is a pretty game for the owners – what fools to keep such a fool on board such a fine vessel.

▷ There is a copy of a letter from Robert Cooper of 12 Harp Lane, City of London, to Captain S. Fowler of Weymouth who, with John Mowlem, was probably part owner of the ship, about this trouble.

Saturday 29 June: I arrived in Guernsey after a fine passage, *Despatch*, Capt. Babot. Called on Mr John Guilbert and then on Mrs Burley but my reception was very cold, and Mr Burley was more cool than his mother. The great advantage once reaped by them is now merged into our firm, thus the coolness. Envy is far better than pity. I will not often trouble them, should I go to Guernsey. On the Sunday I went to the Methodist Chapel to hear a noted Mr Ware preach. He is, I suppose, a good man, lots of talent, strong mind; and no doubt he has more than once seen Edmund Kean play King Richard III, but this he ought to keep out of the pulpit, for there are still a few left that remember this great man. This genius, he acted his own way, he broke through all opposition and made all Shakespeare's plays his own in his own peculiar way. And though this fire and this madness suited the different parts, this rant does not suit a pulpit – or a person who is modestly religious. Mr Ware would frighten some into their graves. A timid soul would shudder. I should say he was in early life used a sledge-hammer, broke granite, or been a boxer, for he gave such whacking thumps and roared out damnation at the top of his voice, first a whisper inaudible to anyone in the chapel, then you might hear him like mighty thunder.

Monday 1 July: I visited all the quarries sundry times and looked through all the bills for June, went to Court on the 4th and passed contract with Thos. Burgoise for his quarry, paid him 100 pounds, paid the lawyers and Mr Randell. I paid all the men on Beacon Hill and returned on 8th July. I find my friend Randell has bought another hill of stone for me in Guernsey, north of St Sampson's. It is a long cartage but it will some day be worth money. The man, le Maitre, that has sold it asked £400 for it. He now sells to me for £60 currency. This is cheap.

This afternoon the rain came on but we were bent on a Gypsy party to Tilly Whim, the elder John Cole and myself, Susy Burt, Miss Randell, Miss Anne Randell, Mrs Anderson and George Manwell. My poor Susan would have been much pleased had she been in this world. We were very happy and our wet clothes was no drawback as we went to be happy. I saw the brig *John Mowlem* coming into our Bay with coals for Mr Randell, wind N fine. She is from Sean, the Marquis of Londonderry's estate, the first coals of this sort ever brought to Swanage.

The brig *John Mowlem* has commenced delivering her cargo of coals which are very good. Went on board with Mr Rust, George Burt and his son. I dined at Captain Pilkington's with a few of his friends. Found Mr Edward Freeman at my house, my partner's brother, from Brighouse, Yorkshire. Meet in Vestry to consider what measures should be taken to prevent the boys from bathing [presumably naked] in front of dwelling houses in Swanage. Walked through the streets to keep the boys in order. Captain Pilkington gave one of them, a young Hixon, a good thrashing. Worse boys there cannot be than the boys in Swanage, ignorant beyond measure.

▷ William Rust of Hyde House, Kingsbury, Middlesex, brought up his niece Elizabeth Hudson (Mrs George Burt), following her father's death just before her birth in 1815. A Memoir of Capt. Pilkington, R.N., appointed Inspector of the coastguard district had appeared in the Poole and Dorset Herald [3 June 1847].

The *John Mowlem* left in ballast for Guernsey, having delivered 24½ tons of coal at 7/- per ton, all done in 5 days, good work for Swanage.

Saturday 10 August: My poor brother Robert is very ill with his cancer; poor fellow, no man was ever more in the dark in this world than he is. He is gone back from childhood, he is thoughtless, careless of his personal comfort. He is most dreadfully ruptured − worse than any man I ever saw − with a horrid cancer in the very spot. It bleed much. The poor fellow will give up his life − I call it a life lost for want of care. No medical man can assist him. He has never improved from anything I said and his whole life, and his sons are far behind some of the working men in the place. How well off they might have been had they taken the tide at the flood − a chance never to be met with again.

I went to see my brother Robert before breakfast. He was up but looked very pale and unwell. I went on to Hurston for breakfast with Mrs Freeman and her children who are staying at my Hurston House for a few days, then went to see them bathe. It was very rough, the waves broke over their heads. I hope for a fine day as Poole Regatta takes place. We have the steamer *Princess* from Weymouth in the Bay, going to Poole this morning with passengers. The [Town] Cryer is just giving notice that Mr White's office has been broken open and all cash taken away. This is bad in a small place like this.

My brother is very unwell, not able to leave his bed. We have our London letters once more on a Sunday; there are a class of men who would make the world religious but this wont do in 1850. I hope never!

Sunday 1 September: I took possession, at the request of the church-wardens, of a pew, once the property of James Chinchen Esq. I well remember him. He was a stone-merchant and always dressed like a gentleman. So did the stone-merchants of old. What a contrast now, those in my youth wore a clean shirt every day!

Monday 9 September: My brother Robert has been dying all this week and at 7 a.m. he is still alive. It is like a healthy man dying, poor fellow, his frame is very strong, his lungs like iron, but the cancer at the lower part of his person is eating him alive. What a dreadful disease. Poor fellow, he is prepared to die, and bears all his suffering with great fortitude.

Tuesday 10 September: I have to record at this moment that my poor brother Robert is no more. His comfort in the world has been but little. I think he has suffered more than most men.

Sunday 3 November: I have brought a manservant with me, he has been in the Army, he came to me on the last day of October. I hope he will turn out a good man. He has a new suit of clothes £4.5.0., and I have advanced him a sovereign. His name is King, he has a good character.

Tuesday 3 December: My new furniture from Graygoose, Queen St., arrived; nearly £100 worth, very good for the drawing room. I find a leg off two chairs, in carriage. I am vexed at this.

Tuesday 31 December: This last day in the year I have given 21 old men their dinner at the Ship Hotel, Swanage, Lieutenant Hancock at the end of the table. All were happy and a good dinner was before them with one pint of beer each. It was a goodly sight to see the old happy men. The eldest was 85, Joseph Brown. I was the youngest in the room except one, which was George Tatchell.

Wednesday 1 January 1851: I dined at Mr Wilcox with his brother Capt. James Wilcox and his lady. The Captain is the finest man I ever saw, a most noble looking fellow, and will be first rate in the Navy. He is the youngest Captain in the Navy.

Monday 6 January: Mr Jackson said today, had he known I was about to give a dinner to the old men of Swanage *he would have said Grace for me*! Thank you, I said. Now the man that can afford to give a dinner to 21 old men, and a man that never had a friend to give him a dinner but one that God has blessed with health and a little wealth, would be a *poor stick indeed* if he could not say Grace before a few old men with a grateful heart and with as much sincerity as any person in the world. Such a man would be unworthy of God's blessing. How are some men puffed up! The blessing I asked and the thanks I offered were from my very grateful heart.

I offered to buy 55 Cambridge Terrace, Paddington, to give £1000 for the same. My manservant George King is going to leave my house. He has fallen in love with the housemaid that my wife was so partial to. The fellow suits me well, but one of the two that are in love must go. I cannot allow this courting business to be going on before my face.

Wednesday 5 March: H. Degoris is wishful that one of the firm should be at St Sampson's on Saturday next as the men are dissatisfied with the pay, or rather the price. I suppose I must go.

Wednesday 12 March: I arrived safe from Guernsey. The quarrymen had stopped our carts because the price was low, but I paid them all and I think made them happy. The pay day was about £520. A young man landed here from foreign parts with two others and one of them is dead at the Hotel. He is a native of Hanover, having been on the Gold Coast — Accra.

This day Joseph Freeman has a son born, his second son. This will keep up the firm.

Friday 25 April: I have my new kitchen, economical, self-acting roasting-jack arrived today from Messrs Mapleback & Lowe from Birmingham. It is Brown's patent, weight altogether 12 cwts. I have never seen anything so complete.

Fixing new stove in front kitchen all day.

THE GREAT EXHIBITION

Thursday 1 May 1851: This day the Great Exhibition was opened in London by Queen Victoria.

Tuesday 6 May: I am off to London.

Saturday 17 May: Once more returned. I have seen strange sights in London, I scarcely know how to account for my time. I have been twice to the Great Exhibition, to say the least of it it is a wonderful plan. I saw the Queen of England and Prince Albert and Royalty in person. I also saw the Duke of Wellington close to him. He is 82 years of age. He looks well. He is something for the French to look upon and consider the pepper he gave them at Waterloo. I have been very

Paving the Strand, 1851, from the Illustrated London News. A pile of Guernsey granite setts stand ready for ramming.

successful in the Metropolis contracts.

Thursday 22 May: Good news from London. Lots of good contracts. Nicholas Bower came into the Bay here with a large ship or barque he is master of. His mother was sent for whilst in church.

Friday 6 June: I have received a letter from my brother Joseph and his daughter, Mrs Scobie, all well in Rial del Monte. Both letters dated April 4th this year. I see both letters came via New York, from thence by the *Arctic*, steamer, to Liverpool, cost 1/- each.

Thursday 19 June: Yesterday morning I returned from Guernsey where I paid all the men, which amounted to about £800. All went off well. Mrs George Burt has another boy for the firm of John Mowlem & Co. I hope he may be a blessing to his parents.

▷ This was George Mowlem Burt [1851-1919] who married his cousin Emily Arbon, daughter of Susy Burt. Their son became Sir George Mowlem Burt [1884-1964], Chairman of the company.

I wrote to Mr Jardine of Bow Street saying send us a policeman and I will see him paid for one year. The conduct of boys here is so very disgraceful that I am really ashamed, not only for myself but for the stranger. I have my namesake here from Guernsey, son of Henry Mowlem my nephew, who is a fine boy, and to whom I am giving a good education.

I received a letter from Mr Jardine of Bow Street saying he would provide a policeman. How easy it is to confer with a gentleman. I shall call on Mr Jackson on my way to Hurston.

I have made a good collection for our policeman. All will be well now in Swanage for one year. The boys are very rude. My namesake left here today for Guernsey via Southampton. He is very young for such a journey, not 11 years old. He is a fine boy.

Monday 21 July: This day we have our policeman, John Cripps, a fine fellow recommended by David Jardine Esq., of Bow Street. I hope now we shall have peace within our borders.

▷ David Jardine of Weybridge, Recorder of Bath, was a regular visitor to Swanage and took a great interest in its welfare. He paid half the cost [£120] towards the new church clock in 1859, and also erected the stone seat at the summit of Studland Hill inscribed "Rest and be thankful". There is also a stone seat on Peveril downs marked "D.J. 1852". He died in 1860.

Cripps has been to Wareham and the magistrates refuse to swear him – some dispute with Mr Cambridge.

Cripps has been sworn in this morning at the Rectory, Mr Serrell and Mr Colecroft, two magistrates, present. This is now completed and we have a police officer in Swanage.

Fine weather, the boys rather frightened of our man. Nothing new, only an order to land my monument when it arrives from Guernsey, by order of the Treasury, through the kindness of Sir James McAdam. Paid our policeman for the first time, being for one week's service 24/- and sundry other things. Sent a silver watch to George Elliot by the *Lord W. Bentinck* to New Zealand which I intend as a present for him. It is a good one from Selbey, Wareham.

Thursday 14 August: This morning I find the vessel, Cobbing master, in the Bay here from Guernsey with my poor Susan's monument in 85 packing cases, also Henry Bisson and his wife. The husband worked nearly the whole of this granite.

This day we have sent off several cases of granite to Kingston and I have driven there and commenced levelling the foundations. Paid Cobbing for freight £7.15.0.

Commenced with the plinth today and fixed one corner. It looks beautiful.

At Kingston all day, fixing granite.

This day the top piece of my poor Susan's monument is fixed. It is perfect in my opinion, beautifully worked, and will look well after 1000 years. Paid Henry Bisson for his time in fixing monument and expenses back to Guernsey, £10. This is liberal indeed but he would like a little more. I have engaged for George Mowlem, my nephew, to go to London to work for us. I much fear he has not sufficient animation for the great metropolis of the world.

I left for Guernsey and returned September 23rd. Bought a hill of granite about 1½ acres and a quarry adjoining about 8 ft front and one hundred feet deep from the proprietor of the Old Bank, price £50. A good bargain.

Monday 20 October: Captain E. Pilkington left us this morning with his wife and family. The poor have lost a good friend. The new Captain has arrived safe from Scilly, and Mrs Damond has allowed her eldest daughter to die at Hurston House. I find Captain Pilkington fell on the deck of the *Gertrude* and damaged his ribs. I cannot go to Hurston in consequence of the death of this young woman. How strange this is, how rude of the mother to take her daughter there without my leave. I am shut out of my own house. I am much vexed.

I have been to my old residence today with Susy Burt and Miss Rendell. I am myself again. This morning George Burt took away his family with him, making in all eleven persons; what a large family for so young a man. I found some man broke his leg last year in the Commercial Road and is going to bring an action. His claim is only one thousand pounds. I hope he will be disappointed. He is 70 years of age – a good price for an old leg.

Saturday 22 November: William Croft was put into the Blind House last night for striking our policeman; this Croft is a bad character, a bad husband, and a great trouble to his parents.

Saturday 27 December: The week has been an eventful one. On Christmas Eve our policeman, John Cripps, was nearly killed. There was a mob of boys and men to the number of 100, and had it not been for Mrs Melmoth I think the poor fellow must have lost his life. I was half a day yesterday at the Rectory with Dr Wilcox and Mr Serrell taking the depositions of sundry persons respecting the attack. I sincerely hope the guilty will be brought to justice and transported if possible. William Croft is the ring-leader of the party and a worse man there cannot be, he is a bad husband and a drunkard to boot. There are issued 3 summons to appear next Tuesday before the magistrates at Wareham. I was chose Warden of the Glass Sellers Company of the City of London. I had no wish for this but it is according to rotation. I hope I may live to see the day when I may be Chairman.

Susannah Mowlem's monument newly erected in Swanage cemetery (1854), originally at Kingston. In 1868 it also became John Mowlem's tomb. Photographed by B.J.K. Rives.

The idle people about the street are rather more dull today, they fancy there is a rod in pickle for them, and unless something be done to protect the quiet inhabitants of this place, all that can move away from it will do so. I often regret I settled down here

Tuesday 30 December: The rioters of this place were taken before the bench of magistrates at Wareham and fined 50/-. Five were taken to Dorchester but on payment of the fine will be released. William Croft was fined £5.0.0. He ought to have been sent to the sessions. The magistrates don't know their duty. I look at them as a set of old ladies. A fine for the rabble here is of no use. The inhabitants are 500 years behind, and those who sit in judgment are further still.

Wednesday 31 December: This is the last day of the year. I have had the pleasure of giving 22 old men a good dinner. All that were there this day twelvemonth were alive to this day. I close the year with gratitude to God for all his mercies.

☆　　　☆　　　☆　　　☆　　　☆

▷ Of a poor preacher, John Mowlem says:

Whilst he was drawing along, my ideas were in the storm, riding upon the summit of a thunder-cloud, looking into the blue expanse of space, trembling with awe at the mighty hand that did direct the storm and hold me safe from destruction.

Oh God! Open my eyes that I may see and guide others through this life.

▷ And during a dull sermon:

Whilst he was grovelling along in commonplace, my mind was on the stretch amongst the great and mighty works of the Great Geometrician of the Universe; first, floating in space taking the moon and all satellites, then the planets and their attendants, the fixed stars, the comets. Then with this Earth putting them altogether, placing the whole in one vast globe making it one immense body of light and combustion which might have moved for millions of years when at last the Great Maker of all caused this vast body to explode when the planets were fragments, the moons also fragments, and the stars.

Then an idea came across my dark and benighted mind that the comets that are now, which whirl through space, might still feel the effects of the great and mighty explosion. All might be yet gathered together again; and again dissolved. All may fade out, the sun may be dim, the atmosphere, taking advantage of his weakness, rush with torrents, drown that once great light.

This may become a vast unfathomable sea that may boil for ages, toss with angry waves.

Then there would be an almighty Light, the Light of the Maker of the Universe, the light of heaven where the Righteous shine forth. How awful the thought for those that worship not their God, but how cheering to the righteous. May the reader and I be of the happy number.

His envoy:

> *All nature is but art unknown to thee;*
> *All chance, direction which thou canst not see;*
> *All discord, harmony not understood;*
> *All partial evil, universal good.*

> ALEXANDER POPE

John Mowlem in later life, photographed by M.J. de Mouxy.

Index